MUTE VOL II #0 - PRECARIOUS READER

PUBLISHED BY MUTE PUBLISHING LTD

ABOUT MUTE VOL.2

Mute vol. 2 is a new imprint from the publishers of Mute magazine, http://metamute.com

As well as making writing from the Mute website and archive available in print, Mute vol. 2 will feature special issues, projects, and Readers collecting texts from Mute and elsewhere.

MUTE ON DEMAND

Mute is printed using 'print on demand' technology and copies can be ordered for resale (or potlatch re-distribution!) through the Mute website.

Mute can be quickly and cheaply printed for events, meetings, discussions, teaching programmes, or activist gatherings.

Editions can be as small or as large as you like, from 1 copy upwards. We offer a discount of 30% on bulk orders for resale.

Contact us for more details.

Email: orders@metamute.com

www.metamute.com

EDITOR
Benedict Seymour <ben@metamute.com>

DEPUTY EDITOR
Anthony Iles <anthony_iles@yahoo.com>

EDITORIAL BOARD
Josephine Berry Slater <josie@metamute.com>**, Matthew Hyland** <convolute@riseup.org>, **JJ King** <jamie@jamie.com>, **Demetra Kotouza**, **Hari Kunzru** <hari@metamute.com>, **Pauline van Mourik Broekman, Benedict Seymour, Laura Sullivan** <alchemical44@yahoo.co.uk> and **Simon Worthington**

EDITORIAL ASSISTANT
Demetra Kotouza <demetra@metamute.com>

ART DIRECTOR
Simon Worthington

DESIGN PRODUCTION
Laura Oldenbourg <laura_oldenbourg@yahoo.com>

ACKNOWLEDGEMENTS
Josephine Berry Slater through her editorial work on Mute Issue 29 made a significant contribution to the editorial content and direction of this MiniMute edition.

The design of this edition is based on a design template orginated for Mute magazine by **Damian Jaques** <damian@aant.co.uk> of AANTGraphicDesign.

ADVERTISING
<advertising@metamute.com>

WEB SITE
<mute@metamute.com>
Metamute is powered by Campware, content management software [http://www.campware.org], with additional software services by our very own OpenMute [http://openmute.org]

Publishers

Pauline van Mourik Broekman
<pauline@metamute.com>
Simon Worthington
<simon@metamute.com>

OFFICE
Mute, Unit 9, The Whitechapel Centre,
Myrdle Street,
London E1 1HL, UK
T: +44 (0)20 7377 6949
F: +44 (0)20 7377 9520
e-mail: <mute@metamute.com>

SUBSCRIPTIONS
Demetra Kotouza
T: +44 (0)20 7377 6949
F: +44 (0)20 7377 9520
e-mail: <demetra@metamute.com>
web: [http://www.metamute.com/subs/]

DISTRIBUTION UK
Central Books,
99 Wallis Road,
London, E4 5LN.
T: +44 (0)20 8986 4854
F: +44 (0)20 8533 5821

CONTRIBUTING
Mute welcomes contributions of all kinds, articles, visuals or collaborations. Please email <mute@metamute.com> with your suggestions.

Cover: Angelo Rindone, Maternita, poster from the chainworkers' http://chainworkers.org campaign,which promotes the cult of San Precario

Mute is supported by
Arts Council England

ARTS COUNCIL ENGLAND

MUTE PRECARIOUS READER

TEXTS ON THE POLITICS OF PRECARIOUS LABOUR

This Reader collects together texts on Precariousness that first appeared in Mute magazine issues 29 (January 2005) and 28 (August 2004) with writing on the politics of precarity from a number of other sources.

The intention is to present in one small *volume a selection of texts which address the problems and po*tentials of the concept of precarious labour. This Reader reflects something of the current discussion and debate around social precariousness, precarious work, precarious life, and the struggles against this condition.

Mute would like to thank the following authors and publications for allowing us to reproduce their texts:

John Barker, Alex Foti, Frassanito Network, Loren Goldner, Hydrarchist, Anthony Iles, Kolinko, Angela Mitropoulos, Kidd McKarthy, Merijn Oudenampsen, Gavin Sullivan, Laura Sullivan, Marina Vishmidt, Interactivist Info Exchange and Greenpepper Magazine.

Mute Vol II Issue #0

CONTENTS

INTRODUCTION: EXPLORING PRECARIOUSNESS

Sometimes it's hard to tell self-congratulation from self-abasement. ***Not a Proper Job,*** **a temping directory for artists, was launched in London in October at a party** advertised as follows:

If you live a creative lifestyle, you are by definition a member of the 'Not a Proper Job' club. So come join us and celebrate not having a Proper Job. Birds of a feather should flock together!

As Marina Vishmidt observes below in her article 'Precarious Straits', the 'relative autonomy' of 'creative' lifestyles 'is underwritten by extreme dependence': that of other, 'uncreative' casual workers, of everyone else still employed in the old-fashioned, inflexible way, and of the unwittingly wretched 'creatives' themselves. So any celebration of artworkers' quasi-freedom is always also cheerleading for all three kinds of servitude. While no more could be expected from a neo-boosterist campaign backed by Greater London Enterprise, the EU and the European Social Forum, it's strange to find a similar logic at work in a lot of critical discourse on 'precariousness'. In the latest issue of *Greenpepper* (October, 2004), Alex Foti of Chainworkers declares that 'the precariat is to postindustrialism as the proletariat was to industrialism.' This suggests that the messianic historical mission of creative and technical 'brainworkers' somehow enobles and redeems the everyday misery of the hyperexploited 'chainworkers' with whom, in the term 'precariat', they are uncomfortably conflated. 'How', asks Angela Mitropoulos below in her article 'Precari-us?', does the fast-food 'chainworker', who is compelled to be affective, compliant and routinised, not assume such a role of relation to a software programming 'brainworker', whose habitual forms of exploitation oblige opinion, innovation and self-management? How is it possible for the latter to avoid assuming for themselves the specialised role of mediator?

The notion of artists / 'virtuosi' / 'cognitaires' etc. as the vanguard of the precariat is based on the equation of precariousness with irregular or casual working patterns. Yet it's hard to imagine a group of workers better acquainted with their own precarious status than those on the regular assembly lines at Siemens and Volkswagen, recently forced to accept a longer working week for no extra money in order to save their jobs from 'offshoring' within Europe.

The idea of transversal social unity in shared precariousness is closely linked to the insight that 'all life is work', in the sense that value is transformed from labour into capital right across the social field, not just in jobs. But 'all life is work' doesn't mean all work is the same. Far more value can be squeezed out of some kinds of labour than from others: hence the war on 'economic inactivity' waged by governments and employers, a desperate mobilisation to get as many people working (in the traditional sense) as many hours as possible. Pious identification between violently stratified social subjects does nothing whatsoever to undermine this war effort.

Menu 2

Alopecia Feast

Starter: Bring your own prawn cocktail
RSI Steak

Eczema Gratin

Desert options:
Glaxo Glacé

Seroxat Surprise

Menu 3

Death By Delivery :

Tacograph take-me-out
Congestion Zone Crunch
Jam

Yorkie bar (8pcs)

Menu 4

Misery Meal (finger loosin' good)

Bonus point Burger
Banana Split-Shift
Sacrificial Shake
Multi-task Muesli
Warning your meal may be poisoned for training purposes

Menu 5

Call Centre Crush

Idle Time King Wing
Pin Code Pina Colada
Overwork Omlette
Served between 3-7 am - standing room only

Menu 6

Postmodern Chicken Farm

Dormitory Delight - half pay, half bed, full insomnia
Battered Brains (4 pcs)
Leg and breast
Love You Longtime Sling

All prepared with cystamatic care

PRECARI-US?

Does the term precariousness or 'precarity', as applied to the conditions of employment under neoliberalism, provide us with more than another trendy neologism? Angela Mitropoulos examines its use, misuse and associated poliltical horizons

Few could be unaware that an increasing proportion of the workforce is engaged in intermittent or irregular work. But I'd like to set aside for the moment the weight and scope of the evidentiary, those well-rehearsed findings that confirm beyond doubt the discovery and currency of precariousness and which render the axiomatic terrain upon which such facts are discovered beyond reproach. Instead, I would like to explore something of the grammar at work in these discussions. As a noun, 'precariousness' is both more unwieldy and indeterminate than most. If it is possible to say anything for certain about precariousness, it is that it teeters. This is to begin by emphasising some of the tensions that shadow much of the discussion about precarious labour. Some of those tensions can be located under various, provisional headings which bracket the oscillation between regulation and deregulation, organisation and dissemination, homogenous and concrete time, work and life.

There are notable instances of this: consider recent research commissioned by Australia's foremost trade union body, the ACTU, into what they call 'non-standard' forms of work. As reported, most of those surveyed said they would like 'more work.'
It is not clear to what extent that answer was shaped by the research, i.e.: by the ACTU's persistent arguments for a return to 'standard hours,' re-regulation, or their more general regard for Fordism as the golden age of social democracy and union organisation. 'Non-standard work' has mostly been viewed by unions as a threat, not only to working conditions but, principally, to the continuing existence of the unions themselves.

But what is clear is that the flight from 'standard hours' was not precipitated by employers but rather by workers seeking less time at work. This flight coincided with the first wave of an exit from unions. What the Italian Workerists dubbed 'the refusal of work' in the late 1970s had its anglophone counterpart in the figure of the 'slacker'. This predated the 'flexiblisation' of employment that took hold in the 1980s. The failure of this oppositional strategy nevertheless provoked what Andrew Ross has called the 'industrialisation of bohemia'. Given that capitalism persisted, the flight from Fordist regularity and full time work can be said to have necessitated the innovation and extension of capitalist exploitation – much like gentrification has followed university students around suburbs and de-industrialising areas since the 1970s.

The search for a life outside work tended to reduce into an escape from the factory and its particular forms of discipline. And so, perhaps paradoxically, this flight triggered an indistinction between work and life commensurate with the movement of exploitation into newer areas. This is why the answer of 'more work' now presents itself so often as the horizon of an imaginable solution to the problem of impoverishment and financial instability – not more money or more life outside work, but more work.

Take the distinction between work-time and leisure-time. These categories become formalised with Fordism, its temporal rhythm as measured out by the wage, clock and assembly line, and distinguished by a proportionality and particular division of times, as in the eight hour day and the five day week. Here, leisure-time bears a determined relationship to work – as the trade-off for the mind-numbing tedium of the assembly line, as rejuvenation, and as temporary respite from the mind-body split that line-work enforces. Yet leisure time was, still, substantively a time of not-work.

By comparison, while the perpetually irregular work of post-Fordism might, though not necessarily, decrease the actual amount of time spent doing paid work, it nevertheless enjoins the post-Fordist worker to be continually available for such work, to regard life outside waged work as a time of preparation for and readiness to work. Schematically put: whereas Fordism sought to cretinise, to sever the brains of workers from their bodies so as to assign thought, knowledge, planning and control to management, post-Fordist capitalism might by contrast be characterised – in Foucault's terms – as the imprisonment of the body by the soul. Hence the utility of desire, knowledge, and sociality in post-Fordism.

The long, Protestant history of assuming work as an ethical or moral imperative returns in the not-always secular injunction to treat one's self as a commodity both during and outside actual work time. One can always try to defer the ensuing panic and anxiety with pharmacology, as Franco Berardi argues. But something might also be said here about that other 'opiate,' the parallel rise of an enterprising, evangelical Christianity; not to mention attempts to freeze contingency in communitarianism, of one variant or another. The precariousness of life – experienced all the more insistently because life depends on paid work – tends to close the etymological distance between prayer (*precor*) and the precarious (*precarius*).

PRECARIOUS SUBJECTS

The term 'Precarity' might have replaced 'precariousness' with the advantage of a prompt neologism; yet both continue to be burdened by a normative bias which seeks guarantees in terms that are often neither plausible nor desirable. Precariousness is mostly rendered in negative terms, as the imperative to move from irregularity to regularity, or from abnormality to normality. That normative burden is conspicuous in the grammatical development from adjective to noun: precarious to precariousness, condition to name.

Yet, capitalism is perpetually in crisis. Capital is precarious, and normally so. Stability here has always entailed formalising relative advantages between workers, either displacing crises onto the less privileged, or deferring the effects of those crises through debt. Moreover, what becomes apparent in discussions on precariousness is that warranties are often sought, even by quite different approaches, in the juridical realm. The law becomes the secularised language of prayer against contingency. This assumes a distinction between law and economy that is certainly no longer, if it ever was, all that plausible. It is not clear, therefore, whether the motif of precariousness works to simply entice a desire for its opposite, security, regardless if this is presented as a return to a time in which security apparently reigned or as a future newly immunised against precariousness.

On a global scale and in its privatised and/or unpaid versions, precarity is and has always been the standard experience of work in capitalism

There are nationalist denominations. Precarity (or *precarité*), in its current expression, emerged in French sociology and its attempts to grasp the convergence of struggles by unemployed and intermittent workers in the late 1990s. Most prominently, Bourdieu was among those who raised the issue of a diffuse *precarité* as an argument for the strengthening of the Nation State against this, as well as the globalisation that was said to have produced it. In its far less nationalist versions, the discussion on precarity is marked – sometimes ambivalently and not always explicitly – by the presentation of a hoped-for means of resistance, if not revolution. A renewed focus on changing forms of class composition or new subjectivities may have brought with it an irreversible and overdue shift in perspective and vocabulary. But that shift has not in all cases disturbed the structural assumptions of an orthodox Marxism in the assertion of a newer, therefore more adequate, vanguard. Names confer identity as if positing an unconditional presupposition. Like all such assertions, it is not simply the declaration that one has discovered the path to a different future in an existing identity that remains questionable. More problematically, such declarations are invariably the expression and reproduction of a hierarchy of value in relation to others.

For instance, if Lenin's Party, defined as the figure of the 'revolutionary-intellectual', paid homage to the mind-body split of Fordism and Taylorism (where others were either cast as a 'mass' or, where actively oppositional, 'counter-revolutionaries'), to what extent has the discussion on precarious labour avoided a similar duplication of segmentation and conformism? Or, to put the question in classical Marxist terms: to what extent can an identity which is immanent to capitalism (whether 'working class' or 'multitude') be expected to abolish capitalism, and therefore its very existence and identity? Does a politics which takes subjectivity as its question and answer reproduce a politics as the idealised image of such? A recourse to an Enlightenment Subject replete with the stratifications which presuppose it, and ledgered according to its current values (or valuations), not least among these being the distinction between paid and unpaid labour.

Let me put still this another way: the discussion of the precarious conditions of 'creative labour' and the 'industrialisation of bohemia' tends to restage a manoeuvre found in Puccini's opera *La Boheme*. Here, a bunch of guys (a poet, philosopher, artist and musician) suffer for their art in their garret. But it is the character of Mimi – the seamstress who talks of fripperies rather than art – who furnishes Puccini and our creative heroes with the final tragedy with which to exalt that art as suffering and through opera. The figure of the artist (or 'creative labourer') may well circulate, in some instances, as the exemplary figure of the post-Fordist worker – precarious, immaterial and so on – but this requires a moment in which the precarious conditions of others are declared to be a result of their 'invisibility' or 'exclusion'.

For what might turn out to have been the briefest of political moments, the exemplary figure of precariousness was that of undocumented migrant workers, without citizenship but nevertheless inside national-economic space, and precarious in more senses than might be indicated by other uses of the word. And, far from arriving with the emergence of newer industries or subjectivities, precarious work has been a more or less constant feature of domestic work, retail, 'hospitality,' agriculture, sex work and the building industry, as well as sharply inflecting the temporal and financial arrangements which come into play in the navigation of child-rearing and paid work for many women. But rather than shaking assertions that the 'precariat' is a recent phenomenon, through the declaration that such work was previously 'invisible', the apprehension of migrant,

'Third World' and domestic labour seems to have become the pretext for calls for the reconstruction of the plane of visibility (of juridical recognition and mediation) and the eventual circulation and elevation of the cultural-artistic (and cognitive) worker as its paradigmatic expression. The strategy of exodus (of migration) has been translated into the thematics of inclusion, visibility and recognition.

On a global scale and in its privatised and/or unpaid versions, precarity is and has always been the standard experience of work in capitalism. When one has no other means to live than the ability to labour or – even more precariously, since it privatises a relation of dependency – to reproduce and 'humanise' the labour publicly tendered by another, life becomes contingent on capital and therefore precarious.

Why exactly is it important to search for a device by which to unify workers – however plurally that unity is configured?

The experience of regular, full-time, long-term employment which characterised the most visible, mediated aspects of Fordism is an exception in capitalist history. That presupposed vast amounts of unpaid domestic labour by women and hyper-exploited labour in the colonies. This labour also underpinned the smooth distinction between work and leisure for the Fordist factory worker. The enclosures and looting of what was once contained as the Third World and the affective, unpaid labour of women allowed for the consumerist, affective 'humanisation' – and protectionism – of what was always a small part of the Fordist working class. A comparably privileged worker who was nonetheless elevated to the exemplary protagonist of class struggle by way of vanguardist reckonings. Those reckonings tended to parallel the valuations of bodies by capital, as reflected in the wage. The 'lower end' of the (global) labour market and divisions of labour – impoverishment, destitution or a privatised precariousness – were accounted for, as an inherent attribute of skin colour and sex, as natural. In many respects, then, what is registered as the recent rise of precarity is actually its discovery among those who had not expected it by virtue of the apparently inherent and eternal (perhaps biological) relation between the characteristics of their bodies and their possible monetary valuation – a sense of worth verified by the demarcations of the wage (paid and unpaid) and in the stratification of wage levels.

BIOPOLITICAL ARITHMETIC

To be sure, there are important reasons to continue a discussion of precarious labour and precarity, of how changes to work-time become diffused as a disposition. Precarity is a particularly useful way to open a discussion on the no longer punctual dimensions of the encounter between worker and employer, and how this gives rise to a generalised indistinction between the labour market, self, relationships and life.

The more interesting aspect of this discussion is the connection made between the uncertainty of making a living and therefore the uncertainty of life that is thereby produced in its grimly mundane as well as horrific aspects: impoverishment, as both persistent threat and circumstance; the 'war on terror'; the internment camps; 'humanitarian intervention', and so on. In this, the topic of biopolitics re-emerges with some urgency – or rather this urgency becomes more tangible for that privileged minority of workers (or 'professionals') who were previously unfamiliar with its full force. Impoverishment and war pronounce austere verdicts upon lives reckoned as interchangeable and therefore at risk of being declared superfluous. What does it means to insist here, against its capitalist calculations, on the 'value of life'?

This raises numerous questions. What are the intersections between economic and political-ethical values? Does value have a measure, a standard by which all values (lives) are calculated and related? Transformed into organisational questions: how feasible is it to use precarity as a means for alliances or coalition-building without effacing the differences between Mimi and the Philosopher, or indeed reproducing the hierarchy between them? Is it in the best interests for the maquiladora worker to ally herself with the fashion designer? Such questions cannot be answered abstractly. But there are two, perhaps difficult and irresolvable questions that might be still be posed.

First, what are the specific modes of exploitation of particular kinds of work? If the exploitation and circulation of 'cognitive' or 'creative labour' consists, as Maurizio Lazzarato argues, in the injunction to 'be active, to communicate, to relate to others' and to 'become subjects', then how does this shape their interactions with others, for better or worse? How does the fast food 'chainworker', who is compelled to be affective, compliant, and routinised not assume such a role in relation to a software programming 'brainworker', whose habitual forms of exploitation oblige opinion, innovation and self-management? How is it possible for the latter to avoid assuming for themselves the specialised role of mediator – let alone preening themselves in the cognitariat's mirror as the subject, actor or 'activist' of politics – in this relationship? To what extent do the performative imperatives of artistic-cultural exploitation (visibility, recognition, authorship) foreclose the option of clandestinity which remains an imperative for the survival of many undocumented migrants and workers in the informal economy?

Secondly, why exactly is it important to search for a device by which to unify workers

– however plurally that unity is configured? Leaving aside the question of particular struggles – say, along specific production chains – it is not all that clear what the benefits might be of insisting that precarity can function as this device for recomposing what was in any case the fictitious – and highly contested – unity of 'the working class'. To be sure, that figure is being challenged by that of 'the multitude', but what is the specific nature of this challenge?

Ellen Rooney once noted that pluralism is a deeper form of conformism: while it allows for a diversity of content, conflict over the formal procedures which govern interaction are off-limits, as is the power of those in whose image and interest those rules of interaction are constituted. Often, this arises because the procedures established for interaction and the presentation of any resulting 'unity' are so habitual that they recede beyond view. Those who raise problems with them therefore tend to be regarded as the sources of conflict if not the architects of a fatal disunity of the class. A familiar, if receding, example: sexism is confined to being a 'women's issue', among a plurality of 'issues,' but it cannot disrupt the form of politics.

What then is the arithmetic of biopolitics emerging from the destitution of its Fordist forms? If Fordist political forms consecrated segmentations that were said to inhere, naturally, in the difference of bodies, then what is post-Fordism's arithmetic? Post-Fordism dreams of the global community of 'human capital', where differences are either marketable or reckoned as impediments to the free flow of 'humanity' as – or rather for – capital. In short, political pluralism is the idealised version of the post-Fordist market.

It might be useful here to specify that commodification does not consist in the acts of buying and selling – which obviously predate capitalism. Rather, commodification means the application of a universal standard of measure that relates and reduces qualitative differences – of bodies, actions, work – according to the abstract measure of money. Abstract equivalence, without its idyllic depictions, presupposes and produces hierarchy, exploitation and violence. Formally, which is to say juridically: neither poor nor rich are allowed to sleep under bridges.

What does it mean, then, to argue that the conditions of precarious workers might be served by a more adequate codification of rights? It does not, I think, mean that our conditions will improve or, rather, be guaranteed by such. Proposals for 'global citizenship' by Negri and Hardt are predated by the global reach of a militaristic humanitarianism that has already defined its meaning of the convergence between 'human rights' and supra-national force. Similarly, a 'basic income' has already been shown, in the places it exists such as Australia, to be contingent upon and constitutive of intermittent engagements with waged work, if not forced labour, as in work-for-the-dole schemes. The latter policy was applied to unemployed indigenous people before it became a recent measure against the unemployed generally. Basic incomes do not suspend the injunction to work often in low paid, casual or informal jobs; they are deliberately confined to levels which provide for a bare life but not for a livelihood. The introduction of work-for-the-dole schemes indicate that, where 'human capital' does not flow freely as *such*, policy (and pluralism) will resort to direct coercion, cancelling the formally voluntary contract of wage labour. The introduction of the work-for-the-dole scheme for indigenous people in Australia followed on the collapse in their employment rates after the introduction of 'equal pay' laws. Their 'failure to circulate' was explained as an inherent, often biological, attribute (chiefly as laziness) and, therefore, the resort to forced labour was rendered permissible by those politicians who most loudly proclaimed their commitment to multiculturalism and the reconciliation of indigenous and 'settler' Australians.

So, how might it be possible to disassociate the value of life from the values of capital? Or, with regard to the relation between a globalised nationalism and aspirations for supra-national arrangements: how to sever the various daily struggles against precariousness from the enticements of a global security-state? Rights are not something one possesses – even if many of us are reputed, by correlation, to possess our own labour in the form of an increasingly self-managed or self-employed exploitation. Rights, like power, are exercised, in practice and by bodies. As juridical codes, they are both bestowed and denied by the state, at its discretion. There are no guarantees and there will always be a struggle to exercise particular rights, irrespective of whether they are codified in law. But, as a strategy, the path of rights means praying that the law or state might distribute rights and entrusting it with the authority and force to deny them.

That said, precarity might well have us teetering, it might even do so evocatively, for better and often worse, praying for guarantees and, at times, shields that often turn out to be fortresses. But it is yet to dispense with, for all its normative expressions, a relationship to the adjective: to movement, however uncertain. 'Precarious' is as much a description of patterns of worktime as it is the description, experience, hopes and fears of a faltering movement – in more senses than one, and possibly since encountering the limits of the anti-summit protests. This raises the risk of movements that become trapped in communitarian fears or in dreams of a final end to risk in the supposedly secure embrace of global juridical recognition. Yet, it also makes clear that a different future, by definition, can only be constructed precariously, without firm grounds for doing so, without the measure of a general rule, and with questions that should, often, shake us – particularly what 'us' might mean.

Angela Mitropoulos <s0metim3s@optusnet.com.au> sometimes produces websites http://antimedia.net/xborder http://woomera2002.antimedia.net http://flotilla2004.com, writes on border policing and class composition, and sometimes comes across a wage

CHEAP CHINESE

The perilous and exploitative employment of economic migrants, despite the public outcry against it, is an essential component of capitalist productivity. Concentrating on the structural insecurity of Chinese workers both in the UK and mainland China, John Barker moves from the contextless media coverage of specific deaths to the macro economic picture that caused them

In June of 2000, 58 Chinese people died of mass suffocation in the container of a lorry that arrived on a ferry at Dover. They died trying to enter the UK illegally. The direct cause of these deaths was the blocking of the container's air vents by the driver, a Dutchman called Perry Wacker. He is the worst of criminals; a panicker lacking the basic nerve required and, in this case, cutting the air supply for fear of being caught. The reporting of the case by large sections of the British media was either downright callous or sympathetic in abstract terms only, the horror felt from putting ourselves in the shoes of those who died proved to be too much.

In early February 2004, 19 Chinese workers who had entered the UK illegally died by drowning on the dangerous shoreline of Morecombe Bay, Lancashire – sands rich in cockles. This time the reporting of what happened was more sympathetic. Once again the direct cause of their deaths was the reckless and incompetent greed of those employing them. It was reported that one of those who died, Guo Binlong, made a call on his mobile phone to his wife in the village of Zelang near Fuqing City not long before he drowned. He said, 'Maybe I'm going to die. It's a tiny mistake by my boss. He should have called us back an hour ago.'

Heartbreaking, twice over: the tiny mistake, that that's how Guo Binlong saw it, and the futility of the call. All the reporting implied that none of the 19 could read English or perhaps even speak it, and therefore would not have understood the sign up by the beach that said 'Fast rising tides and hidden channels. In emergency ring 999'. Perhaps if it had been read and understood, even as the danger became obvious, there would have been a reluctance to ring 999.

In another case involving a 40 year old Chinese man, Zhang Guo Hua, who entered the UK illegally and who died in Hartlepool after working a 24 hour shift in a plastics 'feeder' factory for Samsung, it was in no one's interests, as the reporter David Leigh put it, to make a fuss – neither employers nor fellow workers. He was cremated without an inquest. And for Guo Binlong the mobile phone, one of the technological wonders of the present era of globalisation, that allowed a phone call from the darkness of Morecombe Bay, with the cold water rising, to a village in China, was useless to him. In contrast, a young female Londoner was happily saved from sinking mud on the shore of the Thames by using her phone.

The reporting of these deaths though more sympathetic, quickly identified the ruthless and criminal gangmasters as being responsible. Though they have remained largely unnamed the condemnation has been far stronger than in the case of Perry Wacker. The broadsheet papers talked of these gangsters using stolen 4-wheel drives in the same horrified tones that they portray loan sharks, as if the billions made by the 'high-street' banks belonged to a different moral universe. No, these gangsters were 'tough Scousers with torn jeans' and mixed in with them Triads and Snakeheads.

In the same period as these horrific deaths two other types of Chinese people in the UK are becoming important to its economy: students and tourists. All the students pay full overseas fees of £10,000, and in 2003 there were estimated to be 25,000 students making £250 million for British universities – a fourfold increase in three years. In 2004, the estimate is of 35,000 students. The attractions for British universities is obvious. For the students it offers the chance of a university education when places are so limited in China, and when a British degree is said to look particularly good on CVs. What is certain is that the British government is not seeking to reduce their numbers, even when some also work in the black economy to help pay their way.

In October 2003, it was reported that the EU was expected to approve a new visa regime that will give Chinese people easier access to Europe. Chinese tour groups are expected to be given 'approved destination status'. This almost automatic visa granting would have an in-built safety clause from the EU's point of view in that Chinese tour operators would be heavily punished if any of their clients failed to return to China. This

Photograph : Morecambe Bay, site of Chinese cocklers tragedy, April 2004. Pam Worthington

does not apply to the UK which is outside the Schengen Agreement but is equally keen to receive the money generated by such tourism. This is not negligible. Since 1998 the number of Chinese overseas travellers has almost doubled to 16.6 million. That is only a fraction of its 1.3 billion population, but the prediction is for 100 million overseas travellers by 2020, making them the world's biggest travellers. The UK does not want to be left behind but is seeking watertight agreements with the Chinese government to take back failed asylum seekers and issue new papers to those who deliberately destroy them, an issue the Blair government made much of after the Morecombe Bay horror.

In Britain there is nowhere for the exploited to turn and almost no employers are prosecuted for using illegal migrants

These numbers, and prospective numbers, are another indication of the development of a middle-class in China; middle class in its consumption possibilities that is, or what might otherwise be called a nouveau riche. A copycat nouveau riche highlighted by the recent 'BMW case'. The wife of a rich property owner deliberately ran over the wife of a peasant, Liu Zhongxia, whose tractor she claimed, had scratched a wing mirror on her BMW in Harbin, Heliongjiang province, the heart of North East China's rust-belt, mimicking the Long Island heiress who recently maimed a few in similar fashion after a nightclub entry argument. The driver, Mrs Su, who had also paid someone to take her driving test, was acquitted as no witnesses dared to turn up. That such bad behaviour and the incomes and spending power that allow it now exist is hardly surprising given the dynamic growth of its industrial economy. It can be argued that it is only through the policies of the nationalist Communist Party, determined only to allow in Western capital on its own terms (however much that might be wishful thinking) that this growth has taken place. It is equally the case that it results from the shift of so much industrial production to China from the First World, to take advantage of a low wage workforce, one which is also producing this nouveau riche. The divisions of levels of income and possibilities in China are now so great that they might be called class divisions, and so obvious that the new Communist Party leadership of Hu Jintao and Wen Jiabao have referred to it and of the need to narrow the gap between rich and poor. Beyond the never-ending campaign to root out the corruption of officials and their parasitic relation to the peasantry, this sounds like wishful thinking.

There are not going to be 1.3 billion Chinese in the 'middle-class' level global consumer class. What would they be producing? Even in the 'First World' it is a bogus promise. In the case of China, with such an across-the-board global consumer class, the global environmental crisis would be obvious even to those who do not wish to see it. Instead the situation as it is, and as it is developing, is eminently suitable to the global investor class and its trans-national corporations and companies. As Oscar Romero puts it with the ruthless clarity of 'Third World' analysts, what matters to them is that 'national markets become increasingly liberalised so that they can seek the thin strata with high income in the underdeveloped countries ... they do not aim to sell to the entire population, it would be sufficient for 300 million in the upper-income brackets out of the total Chinese population to become their customers, though this may create a dangerous gap between the two Chinas.' (Oscar Romero, *The Myth of Development*, Zed Books). To manage this dangerous gap, what better than a highly sophisticated one-party state which can maintain a low-wage industrial assembly class, itself privileged from an even larger and lower-waged rural class. 300 million is enough, it dwarfs the present US market.

Taken with similarly proportioned figures in India, this development is a godsend to the global investor class which, as the SE Asian 'financial crisis' showed, was faced with a problem of global over-production. A financial analyst also trading in snappy one-liners, Ed Yardeni, talked of the world needing all the yuppies it can get. Looked at in this light, the Chinese one-party system may be the more reliable given the stunning defeat of the BJP party in India in the recent election; a party which as Arundhati Roy described so well in her essay about the Gujarat pogrom, had sought to manage the 'dangerous gap' with a mixture of neo-liberalism and Hindu nationalism. However chimerical the promises of the Congress Party might be, the election did allow the poor at least to say 'No' to the gap and the way it was being managed.

The poor of Britain and Europe know the present importance of China in particular, life would be that much harder without its prices: a pair of jeans for a fiver or toys for a quid. Its coming importance was highlighted 100 years ago in J A Hobson's *Imperialism*, a book unfairly famous only for having been used and misused by Lenin.

> China seems to offer a unique opportunity to the Western business man. A population ... endowed with an extraordinary capacity of steady labour, with great intelligence and ingenuity, inured to a low standard of material comfort ... Few Europeans even profess to know the Chinese ... the only important fact upon which there is universal agreement is that the Chinese of all the "lower races" are most adaptable to purposes of industrial exploitation, yielding the largest surplus product of labour in proportion to their cost of keep.

Western ignorance seems to have changed little: the Sinology department at Durham University is scheduled to close, and the UK government is to withdraw the small support it gave to those doing M.Phils in Chinese.

Hobson was in no position to anticipate a Communist Revolution or the developing class system of the present. He did however foresee those fears of this industrial development getting out of Western control, manifested in notions of the 'yellow peril' which crop up throughout the 20th century to cause havoc in the minds of the leftist American writers Jack London and John dos Passos. 'It is at least conceivable that China might so turn the tables upon the Western industrial nations, and, either by adopting their capital and organisers or, as is more probable, by substituting her own, might flood their markets with her cheaper manufacturers, and refusing their imports in exchange might take her payment in liens upon their capital, reversing the earlier process of investment until she gradually obtained financial control over her quondam patrons and civilisers.' Such speculation belongs elsewhere: I don't know, for example, how much Chinese capital is invested in US Treasury bonds, but presumably it figures prominently in the thinking of professional, militarised Western geo-politics. In their considerations presumably, oil figures a great deal. China's 'industrial revolution' depends on it. Last year alone its oil consumption rose by 10 percent, along with what *The Times* (11/6/04) calls the 'rampant demand' from not just China, but India and Brazil too; countries 'continuing to guzzle world supply'. Guzzle! It may well be that the spread of US military bases across the oil-producing world is a product of those considerations.

At the same time Hobson raises another possibility, that 'the pressure of working class movements in politics and industry in the West can be met by a flood of China goods, so as to keep down wages ... it is conceivable that the powerful industrial and financial classes of the West, in order better to keep the economic and political mastery ... may insist upon the free importation of yellow labour for domestic and industrial service in the West. This is a weapon which they hold in reserve, should they need to use it in order to keep the populace in safe subjection.' Hobson himself had seen the use of Chinese labour in the South African gold mines. Although, to our ears he sounds melodramatic and unwarrantably sweeping, nevertheless his considerations do overlap with yet another round of the 'Immigration Debate'. The disparity between the freedom of mobility for capital and non-freedom for labour is mentioned, if at all, and then forgotten as if these really do represent parallel worlds. Instead, the same yes-and-nos go round the carousel. Yes we need some skilled workers; yes, we must rationally look at future demographics and who will be needed to do the work to pay our pensions; but at the same time watch out for bogus refugees who are really economic migrants; watch out for the illegal immigrant. But not too hard.

After the death of three Kurdish workers on a level crossing on their way to pick spring onions in the East of England, it was suddenly discovered there were 2000 Chinese in Kings Lynn as if they had never been seen before. In Kings Lynn! Their deaths were more sordid in the banality of the accident than the thriller-like narrative of Romanian ex-train workers fixing signals so that other migrants could leap onto the Eurostar at obscure spots. The reality of the immigration debate is also more sordid. While the Third World is raided for trained nurses whose training was a cost to those countries, immigration fears are regularly rehearsed. The net result is that so many immigrants live in fear, and this fear is as functional to capitalist economies in the present era as it has been in the past. Migrant workers in Fortress Europe, and especially illegally-entered migrants, are far more likely to accept wages and conditions that are essential to its needs, and which in turn have a knock-on effect on wages and working conditions generally. Racist politicians and professional opinionists have their own grisly agenda, but these are functional to capitalist economies and their household names. The focus of these opinionists on 'failed' asylum seekers who are not allowed to work and, more recently, on a 'flood' of Roma and other Eastern Europeans who can work legally as EU citizens, gives the game away Their spotlight is not on Kings Lynn, a national blind spot. 'Policies that claim to exclude undocumented workers,' says Stephen Castle, 'may often really be about allowing them through side doors and back doors so that they can be readily exploited.' Or, as he put it some 30 years ago, commenting on the repatriation demands of Enoch Powell and other racist politicians: 'Paradoxically their value for capital lies in their very failure to achieve their declared aims.'

Inside Fortress Europe, for the UK in particular with its avowedly American-style deregulation, this process is all too visible. It is the dirty secret of the UK's economic success under New Labour. And they are proud of it, these shadow social democrats; the UK's official trade and investment website boasts of it. 'Total wage costs in the UK are among the lowest in Europe,' it says. 'In the UK employees are used to working hard for their employers. In 2001 the average hours worked a week was 45.1 for males and 40.7 for females. The EU average was 40.9. ... UK law does not oblige employers to provide a written employment contract. ... Recruitment costs in the UK is low. ... The law governing conduct of employment agencies is less restrictive in the UK. The UK has the lowest corporation tax of any major industrialised country.' Recently, Jack Straw has 'defied Europe' as the papers would have it. In a speech to the CBI, he promised that the UK would insist that the charter of fundamental rights created no 'new rights under national law, so as not to upset the balance of Britain's industrial relations policy', that is the one established by previous Conservative governments. In Britain there is nowhere for the exploited to turn and almost no employers are prosecuted for using illegal migrants.

To the extent that media coverage of the horror of Morecambe Bay went beyond fingering tough Scouser gangmasters in stolen 4-wheel drives, it focused on the power of supermarkets in the agricultural sector and their relation to those who do the harvesting – a harvest which doesn't stop for a festival because the operation is non-stop, all year round. Migrant labour is up by 44 percent in the last seven years. Much of it is 'legal' via seasonal agricultural schemes, but of the 3-5000 'gangmasters' who organise this at least 1000 are illegal and give no protection to their workers. But then 'gangmasters' are in effect employment agencies and these, as New Labour like to boast, are the least restricted in the EU.

Despite Morecombe and the ensuing hand-wringing, nothing has changed. In September 2003 the House of Commons committee on the environment and food, chaired by Michael Jack MP, found that the agencies supposed to deal with 'illegal gangmasters' were making no real impact and set out the changes that would be needed. In mid-May 2004, a report by the same committee declared that the government had no clearer picture of the situation, and enforcement action against them had not increased. There had, it concluded, been 'no evidence of any change in the government's approach since last September. Indeed, in some respects, enforcement activity has diminished because of lack of resources.'

The beneficiaries of this, are the 'household' names of Tesco, Sainsbury and the rest, all profiting from this underclass. Andrew Simms describes a situation where 'Long chains of sub-contractors, commercial confidentiality and contractual obfuscation, allow household names to hide behind plausible denials ... we have evolved a system better at hiding, or distancing cause from effect.' This at a time when New Labour has never stopped talking of responsibilities in return for rights, exchange value-business. Those who died at Morecombe are believed to have moved on from Kings Lynn, in all likelihood taking a drop in pay from the vegetable picking rates of a market dominated by the 'high street' supermarkets.

Migrant labour is up by 44 percent in the last seven years

The distancing of cause from consequence, the not-me-guv cry of the rich, the powerful and their portraitists, appear in all their colours in the *Teeside Evening Gazette's* report on a fire at the Woo One factory in the Sovereign Business Park, Hartlepool at the beginning of April this year. It mentioned the death of Zhang Guo Hua but only to emphasise that there was no proof of a connection between the haemorrhage that killed him and his working conditions. He had, it reported, been through the usual kind of work: cutting salads for Tesco suppliers in Sussex; fish-processing in Scotland; and packing flowers in Norfolk. Usual for whom?

The Queen had opened the nearby Samsung plant in 1996. It has a global turnover of $33 billion. When it opened the local MP, Peter Mandelson, wrote an article in praise of the company saying: 'some have the impression that the success of the tiger economies is based on sweatshop labour. This is a false picture.' The false picture is that sweatshop labour is exclusive to the 'tiger economies'. Zhang Guo Hua worked a 24-hour shift in Hartlepool. It was his decision of course, one can hear the not-me-guv voice saying. Woo One, the company Zhang Guo Hua worked for, was a 'feeder' factory for Samsung, its practices its own, as Samsung would have it. Zhang Guo Hua spent his last 24 hours stamping the word SAMSUNG onto plastic casings either for microwave oven doors or computer monitors, on his feet throughout. When he collapsed and went to hospital it was under another name. It was only when he was dead that a friend gave Zhang's real passport. So that even though he was cremated without an Inquest, it was in his own name.

An ex-worker at Woo One said that the minimum working week was 72 hours and the minimum shift 12 hours. Its managing director, Keith Boynton, agreed that English workers were not required to work these hours, but it wasn't him guv, the Chinese workers were *technically* employed by an outfit called Thames Oriental Manpower Management with offices in New Malden Surrey close to Samsung's corporate HQ. Thames Oriental Manpower Management – a name that could only have been dreamed up by its proprietor a Mr Lin, not a tough Scouser in ripped jeans but a man who had been granted asylum claiming, claiming that is, that he was a North Korean refugee. Mr Boynton of Woo One said that 'What he (Mr Lin) pays the workers is up to him.' Mr Lin, it was reported had also taken control from Woo One of the nearby three-to-a-room set of dormitories and presumably, because he is now the villain, charged what he liked.

At this time Samsung boasted of record UK factory profits through 'unit cost reduction.' To get some idea of the process whereby this might happen, two pieces of Marx's structural economic analysis come to mind. He had for one thing de-constructed the notion of productivity long before the era of productivity deals. The very notion is one which exactly distances cause from consequence, or rather, and all the more modern for that, muddies the cause. 'Productivity' smears together: the productiveness of labour, that is the improved technology which allows for greater production; intensity of labour, which is how hard people work per hour (and here much of the improved technology simply increases the intensity of labour); and the length of the working day. These latter two factors are characteristic of 'primitive accumulation', and boy was that going on in Samsung's Hartlepool circus. Marx's misnamed Equalisation of Profit Law describes the mechanism whereby this works. The surplus or profit engendered by companies like Woo One, does not all go to them; the size of Samsung, the concentration of capital involved, and its power in relation to both its suppliers and marketing, means that it takes the lion's share of what has truly been accumulated in primitive fashion by small dependent suppliers. This is not some one-off phenomenon; one study shows Toyota having some 47,000 small firms working for it in a hierarchical structure, with most of those in the lowest layer passing the surpluses of 'primitive accumulation' up the chain to transnational corporations like Toyota who benefit from that mystery called 'value-added'.

When the story emerged in *The Guardian* (13/01/04), local MP Peter Mandelson said that he had 'written to Samsung about allegations made against Woo One in this tragic case.' The question is then, did he ever receive a reply because two days afterwards Samsung announced, out of the blue it was said, that it was closing the factory involved – the Wynyard in Billingham. It blamed the high level of wages in NE England and said it was re-locating to Slovakia where wages stood at £1 an hour. To which address did Mr Mandelson write? Was it passed on by a Post Office re-direction instruction. Has he received a reply? It seems unlikely given that Samsung's decision can hardly have been spur of the moment, or that a meeting with Woo One would have been a priority in the two days remaining. It transpired that Woo One themselves had already started to make its own move in the direction of Slovakia, and indeed announced some three weeks later that it was to close its computer casings plant in Hartlepool. On the news of Samsung's departure, Mr Mandelson, his letter still in the post somewhere, said that the price of their product had fallen worldwide, and that was 'the reason for its closure'. Prime Minister Tony Blair said he deeply regretted the loss of jobs involved but that 'It is part of the world economy we live in.'

There are sweatshops in London and Los Angeles even while automatic looms are capable of weaving 760 metres of denim per minute

There is of course much truth in what he says, but there is a complacency to that same voice which talks so much of our responsibilities that grates. If wages in Slovakia are £1 an hour, in China they are likely to be fifty pence, yet there is a need felt in the 'First World' to maintain low-cost mass production within its own frontiers even while its investor class shifts production to such countries. There is for one thing a structural limit to how many lawyers, journalists, IT specialists and bankers are required even in the First World, whatever might be said about education, education, education, while at the same time an increasing reluctance to cushion the circumstances of the excluded population. For another there is a fear at the psychic level of political economy that if so much industrial production is shifted to different parts of Asia, it will somehow weaken the

West, be both sign and symptom of lazy decadence. More specifically than notions of decadence, there is a need for cheap labour in the First World, within its own frontiers, 'for it means that the South cannot extract monopoly rents for its cheap labour and bad working conditions' as Robert Biel puts it. There are sweatshops in London and Los Angeles even while automatic looms are capable of weaving 760 metres of denim per minute. As Hobson suggested, and the irony stands out in neon, this First World low-cost production requires migrant workers, workers made fearful by an unscrupulous media and political class.

Migrant workers are also essential to low-cost China and its 'economic miracle'. The numbers are hard to establish, 80 million is one estimate, 94 another, of recent migrants from the Chinese countryside, many of whom are also 'illegal'. Many Chinese cities require residency permits while it is these 'peasants' who do the jobs that Beijingers, for example, won't do themselves. And, just like anywhere else, for Albanians in Greece for example, they are accused of being thieves and dirty, while also exerting a downward pressure on local wages. Should there be a shrinkage of economic growth at a global level, these Chinese migrant workers will be the first to lose their jobs. For one thing 90 percent of them work without contracts, according to Li Jianfei, a law professor at the People's University. Even the state-run Trade Union estimates that they are owed over 100 million yen in back wages, but a campaign for repayment is for those with contracts only. Much of this is in the booming construction sector, where non-paying sub-contractors blame large companies underpaying them, the Law of Equalisation of Profit in crude form.

In more classical form this law is also inherent in the condition of the coal mining industry. China's increasing oil dependence is well known, but it is also the world's largest coal producer. Chinese companies are making sizeable profits on legal and illegal mining operations, but at prices to industry which mean the real rates of profit of the consuming industries, often foreign-financed, are even greater. Exerting more pressure on the industry and its highly exploited workforce is central government's demand for more output. At the same time the industry has an appalling safety record; around 7000 miners were killed in 2003. There are promises of more inspectorates and the closing of illegal mines but, in the face of this 'energy crunch', this is likely to remain rhetorical. Safety investment is far less than the announced allocation. The grim reality is that with the retrenching of state-owned industries and the accompanying loss of benefits and pensions, the unemployed and the rural poor have entered the industry in huge numbers and are willing to work for cash in appalling and unsafe conditions, often assisting coal mine owners in avoiding safety procedures to ensure continued employment, as the *China Labour Bulletin* puts it. The death of one man in Hartlepool is hardly on the same scale, but the pressures for 'not making a fuss' are similar.

The wishful thinking of the new Communist Party leadership about reversing the dynamics of inequality looks like mere cynical rhetoric since it doesn't prevent it from maintaining a hard line against any independent worker protests over pay and conditions. A strike over pay at the part Taiwanese financed Xinxiong Shoe Factory in Dongguan city in April of this year resulted in several arrests. The Ferro-Alloy strike in Liaoyang province, involving 1600 workers, resulted in long prison sentences for Yao Fuxin and Xiao; meanwhile the workers are still without retrenchment compensation. In Hubei province, six workers have been arrested and are awaiting trial on charges of 'disturbing social order' after a peaceful demonstration at the Tieshu factory; this after 15 months of peaceful campaigning to recover more than 200 million Yuan in back wages, redundancy payments, workers shares and other moneys owed them by the bankrupt factory's management.

Other workers from the Tieshu factory have been sentenced to terms up to 21 months of 're-education through labour', a punishment which bypasses the criminal justice system. We do not know the extent of prison labour in China but it too is a component holding down general wages and conditions. There is nothing to get smug about, prison labour in the UK is being organised in a much more serious manner than before. The Woolworth's type chain in the North of England, Wilkinsons, is highly dependent on it for its products. A recent piece in *The Economist* (6/5/04) goes further, saying 'Hard-working immigrants transform the prison system'. It describes how Wormwood Scrubs (where a regime of extreme and racist staff violence is still being investigated) is full of cocaine drug mules from South America, and how the prison runs production lines for airline headsets and aluminium windows. The best jobs, it says, pay £25-40 a week 'depending on a prisoner's place on the ladder of privilege (as in all prisons, inmates are paid more for the same job if they behave themselves)'. It goes on to say that 'it is serious money for a third-worlder ... so a steady stream of remittances flows from Wormwood Scrubs to poor countries.' A grotesque conclusion might be that the poor victims of Morecombe Bay would have been better off there.

After the effective and international demonstrations against the World Trade Organisation in Seattle, the unity displayed there, the unity that was most unsettling to the global investor class, was quickly confronted with the sneers of professional opinionists. The many American trade unionists present, they said, had no global consciousness, they were just there to protect their jobs. Their demands for basic standards and rights for workers in the poor world were just a subtle form of protectionism, protecting their privileges. It is true that the Clinton administration would do almost anything to secure free trade deals in American interests, and also that Third World voices have been raised to say that such demands for minimum standards and conditions are aimed at cutting off the only way in which they can develop economically, that is with a monopoly on cheap labour, but it is reasonable to ask in return who and what these voices represent. The 'Third World' is not some homogenous space and the class divisions in India and China are clear to see. Increasing inequality within countries rich and poor, is a global reality.

It is such a reality which gives us a nominally social-democratic and a nominally communist government, both spurning any effective protection of workers. Instead then, why not support those working for better wages, conditions and respect in China for example. Lawyers like Cho Li Tai and the Centre for Women's Law Studies and Legal Services at Beijing University; peasant activists like Li Changping; and most of all those imprisoned for demanding basic rights. For this to mean anything in the UK, a start would be mounting support for the Private Members Bill of Jim Sheridan MP and backed by the TGWU, for a thorough registration of 'gangmasters'. If it were to succeed it would at least remove one pillar of the government's boast of its cheap labour and lightly regulated employment agencies and go a step beyond cursory hand-wringing which was the extent of the response to the Morecombe tragedy. Six months later, in August, it was reported that rival 'gangs' of cockle-pickers had to be rescued from the same sands.

John Barker <harrier@easynet.co.uk> was born in London and works as a book indexer. His prison memoir Bending the Bars was reviewed for Metamute by Stewart Home

THE INSECURITY LASTS A LONG TIME

Anthony Iles reviews the online journal Republicart's issue about 'precarious' labour

Republicart is a multi-lingual online journal, publishing articles on the intersection of activist and artistic projects loosely theorised by its editorial as public art. The site is a container for a number of EU funded projects and research on fairly commonplace themes: cultural networking, public space, and social engagement. However, Republicart's recent issue focusing on the 'Precariat' – a subject it proposes as the new proletariat of informal and casualised labour – arrives at a moment when discussion about the condition of human capital and its capacity for action comprises what the editorial rightly calls a 'concatenation' of theories and practices. 'Precariousness' and 'precarious work' have rapidly become terms for thinking through the collapse of the distinction between labour and non-labour and the expansion of capitalist forms of valorisation over all aspects of life. Precariousness names a situation in which, for an increasing number of workers, temporary, 'atypical', workfare or contract work are the bread and butter served on a plate of social insecurity. Republicart's precariat issue brings together recent material by, and reports on, groups and movements, which adopt the term 'precarious' to describe and theorise their struggle within and against contemporary capitalism. It forcefully advances the idea that the precariat consitutes an emerging social movement, but essentially evades a proper analysis of exactly who is precarious and why.

Precarias a la Deriva's text on the Republicart site, 'Adrift Through the Circuits of Feminised Precarious Work', problematises the condition of precariousness as one in which the negative and positive poles of flexibility are inextricable, the conflict between commonality and singularity constant. Their situation bespeaks both a lack and an excess of 'work', a generalisation of instability combined with the 'cognitisation' of everyday tasks and jobs. They are the first to point to the difficulties of organising on the basis of 'a precariousness which can do without a clear collective identity in which to simplify and defend itself.'

Elsewhere on the Republicart site, in his account of EuroMayday 2004, Gerald Raunig quickly shrugs off the difficulty of political organising per se for the atomised and time poor casual worker. Coordinated between Barcelona and Milan, various species of precarie – chainworkers, intermittents, flexworkers and scientific researchers – occupied the streets and the internet in actions 'against the growing precariousness of life.' In Barcelona, the protest developed out of converging struggles against The Forum, a kind of Neoliberal World's Fair, which encountered formidable resistance from those whose lives it attempted to flatten under a dazzling vision of Barcelona as a city of culture. At the same time, in Milan, the Chainworkers, a group of media and labour activists supporting struggles of the non-unionised, blockaded department stores, employment agencies, malls and fast food chains to disrupt and contest the exploitation and flexibilisation of service, migrant and knowledge workers. The potential for organisation amongst chainstore workers in particular, as Raunig asserts, seems rich in opportunities, sharing as they do wage-levels, standardisation of tasks, and boredom. As the Chainworkers' Alex Foti has pointed out, unlike workers in factories whose employers can shift production elsewhere (outsourcing overseas, etc), their employers are rooted to the site of consumption of the goods they sell, making them an easy target and an ideal point for the generalisation of this kind of action.

Republicart's examples are indications of a social movement in formation, but the figure of the precariat remains a contentious one

Also involved in EuroMayday 2004 and represented on the Republicart site by their text 'The Spectacle Inside the State and Out', the French entertainment workers participating in the Coordination des Intermittents et Precaires have combined the defence of their established legal rights (until recently they received annual unemployment benefits as occasional workers in the arts) with the assertion that they constitute part of a new class of flexible labour. Regarded by the major French unions as an undesirable anomaly, Les Intermittents' challenge to economic determinism and the deregulation of social rights has led to a national debate on the very role of knowledge and culture in France. This debate continues to be elaborated by the research groups initiated across the Coordination des Intermittents. Whilst it remains to be seen whether their actions

Unlike workers in factories whose employers can shift production elsewhere, Chainworkers' employers are rooted to the site of consumption of the goods they sell, making them an easy target

successfully restore their particular form of 'dole autonomy', more importantly they have continued to develop avenues of conflict outside of their initial confrontation with the state in a process Maurizio Lazzarato has called 'a deregulation of conflict.'

Groups such as the Intermittents, Precarias a la Deriva and Chainworkers are working in situations where union support is not an option, but little space is given in Republicart as to why this is so, or how unions might respond to the growing pressure from sectors they have hitherto seen as marginal. Whilst the actions of the Chainworkers and Intermittents do go beyond the tradition of union activism there is little evidence for this here. The examples Republicart draws on are indications of a social movement in formation, but for the moment the figure of the precariat remains a contentious one. If Republicart is positing the precariat as a new kind of proletariat then where is the discussion of the composition of this new class? The site's predilection for artistic examples of precariousness has led them to overlook the work of other groups such as Precari Nati and Kolinko (see Mute issue 28), whose analysis of contemporary labour conditions draws on a much more rigorous investigation of how capitalism contains and exploits the energies of the social body and the various forms of refusal it encounters. Casting the precariat's struggle in terms of battles for better legislation misses the opportunity to investigate the tendency for self-organised (or 'disorganised') labour to develop a more generalised struggle than the demand for employment and social rights, breaking with the capitalist organisation of work altogether.

LINKS

Republicart

http://www.republicart.net

Barcelona Forum

http://www.forumbcn2004.org

and Counter-Forum

http://barcelona.indymedia.org?catergory=forum_2004

Euromayday 2004

http://www.euromayday.org

Stop The Clock, Aufheben pamphlet, 2000, by Precari Nati, Wildcat, Aufheben et al

http://www.geocities.com/aufheben2/stc_intro.html

'L'intermittence et la puissance de métamorphose', Maurizio Lazzarato,

http://multitudes.samizdat.net/article.php3?id_article=1082

Unionising Workshop at Flaxman Lodge

http://flaxmanlodge.omweb.org

Greenpepper Magazine

http://www.greenpeppermagazine.org/

Republicart Precarity issue

www.republicart.net/disc/precariat

Anthony Iles <Anthony_iles@yahoo.com> is variously a writer, librarian, assistant editor of Mute and member of Gratipalis[t]a Sound System http://anomie.omweb.org

PRECARIOUS STRAITS

What is obscured by the identification of the cultural worker as exemplary flexibilised worker or 'precarian'? Marina Vishmidt interrogates the recent fashion for equating artists with other forms of insecure (service) workers who lack their accompanying cachet

In recent years, there have been myriad attempts in curatorial, critical and media sectors to index the characteristics of their fields to the wider structural transformations in the landscape of work. These have mainly been enunciated along the axes of 'creativity' and 'flexibility' once deemed endemic to the artist as constitutive exception to the law of value and now valorised as universally desirable attributes in neoliberal policy statements and their bio-economic implementations. Many of the current tendencies to formulate analyses through the prism of culture as labour have begun to discuss the generality of conditions across fields of social production under the rubric of 'precariousness'. 'Precariousness' as a term strives to evoke all the downsides of the institutional embrace of informality. This embrace occludes the gleeful despatch of Keynesian social contracts or other state mediations of capital's risk, the etiolation of organised labour, and the 'personalised domination' of the deregulated workplace that Paolo Virno discusses in his writing.1 'Precariousness' signals a common thread of instability and exposure in the new landscape of work, shadowing the otherwise disparate life prospects of everyone from illegal service workers to academics and web designers. The real subsumption of social life in 'cognitive' capitalism is granted, and this subsumption has a paradoxical face: the more life is work, the less is work guaranteed to assure the propagation of life. Therefore 'precariousness' marks the real and ideological poverty of capital's subjectification, and, hopefully, the site for a broadly-based contestation of its effects.

As a diagnosis, 'precariousness' seems, well, remarkably flexible, mobile and adaptable. 'Precariousness' has surfaced in a number of recent interventions: at workshops in flagship institutions and in self-organised spaces, exhibitions, screenings and investigative, textual and audio-visual practices emanating from social centres.**2** It has scaled the agenda of European public art research initiative *Republicart*, which devoted a special issue of its web journal to the 'Precariat' in August 2004.**3** There have also been high profile national campaigns resisting the evisceration of legal statutes which recognise the tenuous economic bases of cultural work (Intermittents du Spectacle).**4** Some of these projects, particularly the Unionising Workshop at London's Flaxman Lodge held in June 2004, have moved the debate on from the production of an abstract parity between the reproduction of subjects in the 'social factory' or the threadbare equation of wildly dissimilar types of communication work as 'immaterial labour'. Those discussions also thematised the connection between the production of subjectivity in 'creative work', the refusal of work, and the recomposition of workers as a class autonomous from, if always immanent to, the capitalist social relation, inspired by readings from the 'Italian laboratory' of Antonio Negri and Paolo Virno. There have been some developments in a media activist milieu also, with Italy's Chainworkers**5** setting out to mobilise the plurality of the casualised workforce abandoned by traditional unions by providing legal advice and material facilities, coordinating actions and even the ordaining of a new saint who intercedes for the 'precariat'.

The discernible eclipse of housework, care work, etc. in the cultural turn to 'precariousness' ... risks embedding itself precisely in the terms that it is interrogating – the dogma of 'creativity'

The account which would have cultural production as exemplary is valid insofar as cultural economies spawn the prototypes emulated in most labour regimes that rely on unremunerated and mystified work to ensure the lopsided distribution of profit and prestige, as well as the deployment of 'creativity' to soft-pedal submission to these regimes. In that light, the artist or information worker is a model precarian, traversed as she is by intangible demands to commodify the very routines of her survival and the very idiom of her critique. However, what may also be instructive in the uses of 'precariousness', especially those that try to critically appropriate the figure of the artist as the ideal pliant and omni-creative subject of capital, is the omission of the ordinary invisibility that always sustained the free movement of capital, Keynesian or networked: the flexible, informal, spontaneously value-adding sites of housework, personal care, seasonal and surreptitious labour – the disposable labour that was always at the core of the process if not the narrative of accumulation. The discernible eclipse of housework, care work, etc. in the cultural turn to 'precariousness', not only misses a whole swathe of the substance of 'relational' or 'affective' capitalism, but risks embedding itself precisely in the terms that it is interrogating – the dogma of 'creativity'. Whereas at one time domestic work was excluded from Marxian theory on the basis of its exclusion from the exchange of abstract labour power, as mere 'reproduction', nowadays it is excluded from critiques of emergent forms of labour not just because it is not considered 'creative', not just because it is unpaid, but because 'creativity' supplies an alibi to an ossification of social and productive relations which cannot admit, let alone imagine, the challenge posed by the destruction of housework as a discrete activity.

Certainly, there have been sociological forays into the resurgence of (under)paid domestic work,**6** and Precarias a la Deriva have allocated much of their research to the ongoing invisibility of care work as the motor of restructured and informationalised capital, with a focus on the preponderance of women in 'precarious' sectors *such* as housework, *such* as call centres. Nonetheless, the discursive emergence of the term 'precariousness' to denote a shift away from 'immaterial labour' as both too precise and too constraining a descriptor, has often entailed an emphasis of the cultural worker as the salient of precariousness. Yet we do not need to strain to see that 'precariousness' has more to do with a generalised seepage into the working world of the kind of informal and mundane degradation formerly confined to the corridors of labour without value, labour without sociality, labour without end – domestic labour.

> We pose, then, as foremost, the need to break this role of housewife the chrysalis in the cocoon that imprisons itself by its own work, to die and leave silk for capital.
>
> Mariarosa Dalla Costa

In her 1971 text *Women and the Subversion of the Community*, Mariarosa Dalla Costa proposes that the marginalisation of women's labour in housework presupposes the division and organisation of labour in capitalism as a whole. The housewife is the archetypal privatised industry, providing services that could and should be socialised. If capital relies on the family to compensate for the psychic, social and economic antagonisms of paid work, if the family is the locus of reproduction of labour power and its discipline, then the refusal of capitalist family structures amounts to refusal of work tout court. Women are thus uniquely situated to contaminate the whole of society with their struggle for self-determination – a struggle that is irreducible to securing 'fulfilling' work outside the home. While it would be slightly tendentious to transplant this analysis unmodified into a present at least marginally inflected by the capillary action of 30-odd years of feminism, the articulation of invisible and naturalised exploitation inseparable from the production of surplus value still holds, in a social field both stratified and homogenised by such production. Housewives, yes, but also children, migrants, prisoners, welfare recipients, the elderly, the demented, the drivers and the passengers of buses. It is crucial to note here that production of value does not automatically translate into the site of conflict, otherwise Dalla Costa would be fêted as one of the pioneers of cultural studies. It is housework and childcare that, as neglected site of production of value, is also a neglected site of conflict, as it is pivotal to accumulation. In staunch biopolitical terms, the family as control centre of life is thereby the control centre of productive potential.

Dalla Costa's analysis may also be leveraged to expose another dissymmetry in the adequation of cultural life forms with precariousness: the function of discipline in the production of subjectivity specific to the social arena in question. The disciplinary function of the family is well-rehearsed; the disciplinary function of culture is perhaps a bit more esoteric, bracketing as it does the image of culture as emancipatory. But this is precisely what calls for scrutiny in the formulation of the artist as precarious worker. Culture/art is a tremendous disciplinary idiom in Western societies, and this is instantiated around us in ways as imperceptible as they are ubiquitous. The prominence of community art and cultural regeneration in rural and urban responses to deindustrialisation is relevant here. Community or socially engaged art tends to showcase the same defusion of antagonisms that the family once played host to, a safe space to be creative without reimbursement or real-world consequences of any kind (except for the art professionals of course). What discourses of precariousness in art worlds can alert us to, if at other times dissemble, is art's status as a commodity relation, and that its relative autonomy is underwritten by extreme dependence. In this sense any radicalisation of the art relation in the discourse of precariousness and becoming-precarious needs to concede its disutility as a paradigmatic case; at best it reflects or shares some of the earmarks of working life – isolation, anxiety, opportunism. The formula of the artist as a model precarian dissembles what is most at stake in the production of precariousness: the stratification of social production and the imposition of work. A more suggestive formula might be the artist or art worker as vanishing mediator of capital, vanishing precisely in their imaginary negation of its laws.

Perhaps what is more interesting, and potentially challenging, than the projection of similarities between the insecurity of cultural work and the insecurity of shitwork is a complex awareness of incongruities between these. It is one thing to note that the reconfiguration of work has traumatic repercussions across social fields; but these repercussions are not haphazard. The problematic nature of much activist-inspired or 'engaged' art is that it wants to generalise the conditions of art-making to the social without realising that it is as inescapably caught in the social logic it wants to disrupt. Perhaps a way around this would be to focus on the singularity of arts structures, stable and shifting, and the kind of critique this specificity engenders. What kind of singularity can impair functionality? The experimental features of art as an activity are always mitigating against its economic overdetermination as social field. The unrepresentability of contemporary configurations of work and politics, the readiness to spurn existing subjective dispositions in favour of not-yet existing or as-yet malformed techniques of thinking and becoming, may evoke this singularity.

A purposeful engagement with uselessness characterises art *in principle*, and this also marks the potential of constituting other forms of life on the basis of the loss of measure theorised by some as the innovation of post-Fordist work. What a loss of measure could imply for cultural production is that culture can no longer be relied upon to supply an alibi to other forms of work. But since disparate kinds of work produce different kinds of value, all work cannot be subsumed into culture.

Like everything else nowadays, art doesn't produce anything. This uselessness can be mobilised constitutively; there is still a great schism between uselessness and irrelevance to be exploited. Against the instrumentalisation of art and the instrumentalisation of its critique in the discourse of creativity, how far can we go with grasping a specificity that can be resistant to this, the specificity of the already existing and not-yet at once? This might be what is really precarious about art; the oscillation between what it can do as social production and how it is deployed as 'social engagement'. Without this recognition, the appropriation of precariousness in art worlds risks becoming another bad-faith eulogy to the lost dream of bohemia, rendered in the muted palette of the service industries.

FOOTNOTES

1 Paolo Virno, A Grammar of the Multitude, Semiotext(e) / Foreign Agents, MIT, 2004

2 Atelier EUROPA, a symposium and exhibition for the Munich Kunstverein, March 2004, http://www.ateliereuropa.com/; Unionising Workshop at Flaxman Lodge, a week of research, screenings, discussion and production, London, June 2004, http://flaxmanlodge.omweb.org/modules/newbb/viewtopic.php?topic_id=23&forum=11; Precarias a la Deriva, an initiative between research and activism arising from the feminist social center La Eskalera Karakola in Madrid http://www.sindominio.net/karakola/precarias.htm; Producta, a series of events in Barcelona April 2003, http://www.yproductions.org/producta1_e.html and http://www.yproductions.org/proyectos/Producta1_sinopsis_ingles.pdf

3 http://www.republicart.net

4 http://www.intermittents-danger.fr.fm/ The literature of the Intermittents campaign is full of references to the indispensability of healthy culture industries for European tourism and profitability in general. While this indicates a perhaps judicious pragmatism in their campaign, it does detract from the potential expansion of the campaign beyond cultural workers, and it also swerves from critiquing the whole concept of a 'cultural exception' and how such an exception is maintained

5 http://www.chainworkers.org

6 Publications include Servants of Globalization: Women, Migrants and Domestic Work by Rhacel Salazar Parreñas, Doing the Dirty Work: The Global Politics of Domestic Labour by Bridget Anderson, and Global Woman: Nannies, Maids, and Sex Workers in the New Economy, eds. Barbara Ehrenreich and Arlie Russell Hochschild

Marina Vishmidt <maviss@blueyonder.co.uk> is a writer, lapsed film-maker and researcher

PRECARITY AND N/EUROPEAN IDENTITY

An interview with Alex Foti (ChainWorkers) by Merijn Oudenampsen and Gavin Sullivan

This interview took place in July 2004 at the Mill Squat in Amsterdam, during the period it was liberated from the destiny of selling 'traditional' Dutch paraphernalia to tourists. Merijn Oudenampsen and Gavin Sullivan from *Greenpepper* magazine (Amsterdam) spoke with Milan-based organiser Alex Foti - formerly of the Italian flexwork syndicate ChainWorkers [www.chainworkers.org] - about precarity, European labour conflict, and the spread of new syndicalist modes of subvertised collective action across Neuropa. Alex Foti is the Guest Written Editor of the Precarity issue of *Greenpepper* magazine.

Greenpepper: Alex, can you introduce yourself, and the ChainWorkers?

Alex Foti: I am a union and media activist from Milan, Italy and have been part of the ChainWorkers CreW since its inception in 1999 - 2000. Most noteworthy, we are associated with the MayDay parade - which this year reached its fourth edition, bringing around 100,000 temp workers, part-timers freelancers and other types of non-standard workers onto the streets in a joyful (but angry) expression of dissent around sub-standard conditions of work and living. This year the MayDay parade took the form of a major picket line throughout the shopping arteries of Milan. In fact, within the city limits of Milan, no major chain store or retail outfit was open for trading – either because they had become scared by the campaign we had developed in the months prior to MayDay, or because of the flying pickets that 2000-3000 people did in the morning prior to the start of the MayDay parade. This year, the parade was a EuroMayDay parade because it was done together with sisters and brothers in Barcelona, and organised in assemblies that took place throughout Milan, Barcelona, Rome, and (most crucially) Paris – with the participation of the Intermittents: the temp stagehands and part-time actors that recently blocked the Cannes Film Festival.

GP: You have been organising around the theme of precarity. Yet here in the Netherlands we do not really know of this concept. The idea of precarious labour – i.e., dangerous working conditions – is somewhat popularly circulated, but the idea of precarity in itself and the precariousness of life has not yet reached northern Europe. Could you explain what is meant by the term precarity?

AF: In the radical left nowadays there are two major interpretations of the concept. One is existential precarity. That is, that life is precarious in times of global war. Either you are a body subject to bombs and military conflict or you are a prisoner whose habeas corpus is violated in Abu Ghraib or some other Western prison. Wherever there is total domination there is existential precarity.

Precarity is also, however, the condition of being unable to predict one's fate or having some degree of predictability on which to build social relations and feelings of affection. The diffusion of intermittent work and the attacks on the welfare state have resulted in a widespread increase of existential precarity across Europe – affecting increasing numbers of the population even in the wealthy countries like Holland. A clear example of this precarisation is witnessed by the incredible rise in the use of psycho-pharmaceuticals and anti-depressants. Work hours have increased all over the territories – in Europe, the USA and Japan. What is noteworthy is that in Europe, working times have increased. Working on Sunday, Saturday, ungodly hours and night shifts – which previously only involved a small percentage of the workforce – has now expanded and increased. This is precarity: being unable to plan one's time, being a worker on call where your life and time is determined by external forces. And, of course, if you have a sub-standard contract you do not have a full social citizenship. That is what MayDay is all about: claiming social rights for an emergent subject that is crucial to neoliberal production. Neoliberal production is postindustrial – it's service, information, and knowledge-based and we want to get into that. This is at the heart of the accumulation process that is taking place today in Europe and in all advanced capitalist countries. So wherever there are neoliberal chains of production in the five continents, there is going to be precarity – peripheral in terms of rights, but central in terms of the financial web of the creative value produced.

We have been concentrating on two types of workers: chainworkers (being workers in malls, shopping centres, hypermarkets, and in the myriad of jobs of logistics and selling in the metropolis) and what we call brainworkers (cognitive labourers; programmers; freelancers who possess individual value on the labour market but do not yet have a collective force or a subjectivity with social rights – that is, they might make above-standard wages but if they lose their job they are thrown into poverty). Chainworkers, on the other hand, are always on the verge of social exclusion. They are collectively unorganised, but they could organise. What we've been working on is establishing solidarity. That is where media activism comes into play – by supporting strikes, picket lines, sabotage, boycotts on the part of Taylorised proletarianised service workers, and at the same time agitating university researchers, teachers, workers in the information industries and advanced service sectors.

GP: The main idea of precarity, then, is this interminable lack of security. Is precarity then simply defined negatively – as a situation marked by the absence of 'jobs for life' ?

AF: Exactly. While existential precarity is what attracts interest in the issue – because it is lived on the bodies and minds of everybody – we think precarity has more to do with a position in the labour market. It is a post-class discourse, if you like. Previously in this society we were used to blue-collars and white-collars so to speak. Now what we see is a transition to a more unstable social configuration based on service and knowledge labour. In old classist terms, this class exists ex se but not yet per se. That is, it has a clear role in social production, but it doesn't yet have representation of its collective needs – needs of social aggregation, access to standards of sociability, housing, access to knowledge, open source forms of organising, union rights and bargaining rights all around the table. What we have seen is that creative workers do not perceive themselves as workers anymore. The reversal of the new economy exposed the myth that talented people would be protected forever from market fluctuations.

This is what we have to focus on: to fight against exclusion and inequality and bring in a new radical subjectivity and identity in creative productive distribution processes in which social relations and trans-border exchanges are absolutely vital. Especially in terms of the polity on which we want to base our social claims and agitation. We think in Europe today, at the juncture of a global crisis of neoliberalism, there is space for radically organising Eurowide. EuroMayDay is a first step in this process. The migrant struggles are another example of a struggle that is articulating itself on a wider scale. The basic human rights are being written right now and we want basic rights for temps, part timers and migrant labourers to be included on the European continent.

GP: The classical labour movement also agitates around similar issues: full employment, workers' rights, social services, social exclusion, and temporary work. What distinguishes your political agenda (or the radical activity around precarity) from that of the classics?

AF: Full employment is already here. Everybody is working 100 percent of the time – either when they work or when they consume, and display signs, body signs, visual signs, choices. The fact that you wear a particular sneaker or that you write a composition, an email, or mime that becomes an ad. And of course, during the daytime you produce for wage labour. Your data is capital for market research. Your biometric data is capital for biotech firms. We are 100 percent of the time part of the [re]production of capital. In this sense, full employment has already been negatively overcome. I mean, what we need to do is to find ways of social representation that are different from the social democrats and the union parties. Because if Seattle really marks a transition to a new kind of politics – a participatory politics, a biopolitics if you like, in which the old distinction between political work, union work and cultural work is dissolved – then that world is over.

I think that the future lies in developing forms of self-management of conflicts federating themselves across borders and across wider political spaces – from the regional to the transcontinental. As in, a way of expressing political and social claims independently – in the political forms of working with existing radical parties and existing radical unions and associations – yet as an autonomous force. Radical organisations are too stale and backward looking to see what the social mobilisations are that society is asking from us. In France, Spain, and Germany wee see massive amounts of people protesting against welfare cuts and European monetarism (the total right wing European construction made by banking concerns that is keeping social spending low and interest rates high).

All of this activity needs a new form of organisation. I personally think that Anarcho-Green is our output and destination. I think that now that the cold war is officially over on the European continent, we can merge Libertarian, anti-Racist, and Transgender social activism together to create new radical identities that can bring Eastern European and Western brothers and sisters into a new political project capable of opposing fascist Bushism. I mean, this is the task at hand and social conflict is spiralling. Others possibilities are, of course, the peace movement, the open source information movement, the alternative global fair-exchange movement etc. But we need to pose ourselves the question of power and the institutional interface. This is vital at this stage.

GP: One of the things that I noticed in the manifestos that were circulating throughout EuroMayDay this year were new words that we do not know in Northern Europe – like flexicurity. Could you explain what you mean by flexicurity and how that word is activated alongside precarity.

AF: Yes. In fact, in one sense flexicurity means we do not want to go back to a 'job for life' – the system of the previous generation. We accept the flexibility inherent in the computer-based mode of production, but we want to disassociate from the precarity that is implicit in this forced (Faustian) bargain. In the Netherlands, flexicurity is the reality – since in Holland, by law, you cannot discriminate between a part-time worker and a full-time worker in terms of the hourly wage paid. So if we could extend this principle, which is a minimal social claim, all throughout the EU. The fact that part timers cannot organise themselves because they can be fired is, in fact, wage discrimination (with a union discrimination attached). We could also build into this claim a demand for a European minimum wage, ten euros per hour, all across the union. These are the staples – the building blocks of a more advanced, solidarious, less Darwinist society – that could become the 'European model' as opposed to the neoliberal model or to the Chinese or the nationalist capitalist model. Fuck it! I did not choose precarity for myself as a destiny. But I think that out of that condition, our generation – the post cold war generation – can fight for a socially progressive shift. In Spain it is already happening. In the UK it will happen. In Italy it will happen. A shift that can posit a new radical left. Just as the thirties and the forties were times of social experimentation with radical identities, this is the time to invent new forms of cultural imagery. A new imagery of conflict, a new imagery of picketing, a new imagery of social activism. Of course, the media you develop is essential to this task.

GP: As you mention, the theme and discourse of precarity has become a very important organisational vehicle in Italy, Spain and France – with lots of people on the streets for EuroMayDay this year, quite a great deal of material being written and circulated about it, and conferences being organised on the topic. But material conditions in Southern Europe are quite different than those in Northern Europe or the Netherlands ?

AF: Fragmentation and individualisation of service labour is the norm all across advanced capitalist countries – be it Japan, the Netherlands, the UK or Spain. What is different, and specific to Holland, is that the unions were more moderate and in the 1980s struck a bargain to regulate flexibility. Nevertheless, we still see a pressure on the long-term unemployed and a desire to cut benefits all across the board. So I don't at all agree that this is only a Southern European problem.

What is most striking about Southern Europe is that the welfare state there is more backward and traditionally less developed. There is more importance attached to the family and corporatist ways of integration etc. But the tendency toward the reduction of welfare services is universal, and Maastricht is a system designed to keep social spending low. We see that even Germany and France cannot respect these restraints. If we don't act now, we're looking at a future of precarity for all Europeans. Because the idea is to make us a new Asia or a new America – not a new Europe.

OK. I am inviting Dutch brothers and sisters to think about it. Neoliberalism is still very strong. Bolkestein is a neoliberal whose commissioners' mission is to make Europe safe for the US and other global corporations. We are the new workforce produced by neoliberalism. Neoliberalism is managing and governing the construction of Europe. So we are the only credible adversaries and the only guys and girls that can actually block the system of exchange and the flow of information. If young people stop working in Amsterdam, Amsterdam shuts down. No bars can operate; no tourist hotel can operate; no fucking newspaper can be ever produced; no theatre play can operate. Amsterdam is a factory shut for business. This is what Amsterdam says to the world, it is image brand and sociability, which occurs through bodies and minds of thousands of young temps, precarious freelancers coming from all over the world. This is what precarity is – it's both a condition of exploitation and an opportunity.

GP: Precarity as a word to describe the existence in advanced capitalist economies of a fragmented workforce seems very useful and it has undoubtedly been used really effectively in the EuroMayDay events this year – which, as you have said, have seen tens of thousands, or hundreds of thousands of people demonstrating around the theme of precarity. Yet you also mention that there are lots of different types of workers within and under the banner of precarity – extending from unrecognised migrant and feminine labourers towards creative workers working in design and media industries etc.

How useful and effective do you think the concept of precarity can be in linking people together who have vastly different incomes? Precarity seems to be different than blue-collar or white-collar; it seems to be bringing together lots of different types of people from very different social strata. Do you think this is a limitation on how useful the concept might be in creating and organising this new radical subjectivity?

AF: It's a crucial objection and I want to answer with an example that is unfolding before our eyes which is the intermittent struggle in France initiated almost a year ago. What happened was that there was a reform of the unemployment benefit system that excluded thousands of people from maternity leave and other livelihood necessities, especially during the wintertime when the art and culture festival scene is more dormant. What happened then was that these people started blocking all festival productions across France and decided to sabotage the 8 o'clock TV news, breaking into the studios and reading communiques, eventually forcing the issue onto the whole of the cultural intelligence, a much higher class than the intermittent themselves who were mostly stagehands and part-time workers. We have to remember that for every festival there are a thousand workers setting up the stage and that they are cultural workers too. So we saw that film directors and major actors and actresses joined in solidarity with the intermittent cause. And as a result, eventually public opinion started to take an interest. From a discussion on their specific system of unemployment benefit, it quickly became a discussion on the system of unemployment benefits itself. And from a specific discussion about a certain cultural sphere, it soon transformed into a national discussion on the place of knowledge and culture in French society and what kind of rights should be allocated to this sector. In Cannes we saw (Jean-Luc) Godard giving their press conference and Michael Moore expressing solidarity with them. Now the intermittents' cause is known to readers form Sydney to Singapore and New York. What we see here is that from a very specific conflict – through networking and criss-crossing social classes and roles in the production process – the elites and the non-elites, exploited migrants and middle class women, all collectively produced a general shift and movement against precarity.

So precarity rallies different people. As Milanese and MayDay people we think that certain young people, women and migrant workers have a special stake here because they are the social categories being most aggravated by precarity. From another point of view, I think that service industry and knowledge industry – technicians, programmers, cashiers and retailers, sellers, cultural operators, truck drivers and pizza delivery boys – are crucially important. These two very polarised categories are statistically the two sectors that seen the highest growth of employment during the last twenty years of neoliberalism.

GP: So, you don't see this as a phase of pan-capitalism, where the breakdown of the welfare states and social rights are withdrawn as long as the economy is in crisis? Don't you think that when the economy booms again, politicians will be able to circulate around more money, and that salaries will rise etc.?

AF: This system is structural. The sociologist Manual Castells, looking at the last twenty years, saw the precarisation of one quarter to one third of the labour force in advanced capitalist countries as a structural feature. It won't go away with an expansion. If anything, the expansion will simply lure a segment of the knowledge class into the bourgeoisie. But as soon as the boom subsides, there are new additions and the pool of precarious workers will enlarge itself. That's what we've already seen. Italy started in the 1980s with ten percent of precarious workers, a million and a half black market workers.

Nowadays, we have seven million precarious workers (contingent, freelance and temp) and four million black market workers. That's almost half of the total workforce! And it won't go away. Unless – and this is vital for us – we strike on the workplace, we picket the workplace and we manage to get the money: not from the state but from greedy corporations. This is really what organising is all about, that is where the money is.

Who benefited from the dotcom boom? We know: Amro Bank benefited, Nina Brinks benefited, Enron and other guys that where just tricking the accounts. These guys were not making the money; everybody was falsifying the accounts to accumulate financial wealth. Now we see what was behind it all. You see, the problem is, if you keep everybody under the poverty line – as Wal-Mart is doing with its workers – the system collapses. You have to resort to forge and fraud to keep up the system, to keep up financial wealth because you are not selling. Man, this is really a great recession what we are seeing. So nothing will happen unless we organise. There is no easy way out of this system. This is structural. This is historical. It requires a major social shift otherwise it is going to become Brazil all over the world. Already, Holland is a very unequal country – more so than Sweden and Germany. There are very rich elites commanding major amounts of global income. This is what Mayday is about – beating neo-liberalism on its feet and on its territory: global chain stores, global banks, global nodes of finance, global media conglomerates: Murdoch, Berlusconi, Gates.

GP: Many precarious workers are working in areas where there is no self-organising activity. What kind of methods are you using to experiment with organising traditionally unorganised people in these new economic sectors?

AF: We started trying to merge subvertising (as a way of communication) with traditional forms of anarcho-syndicalism – that is, the picketline, the direct action, from breaking the chainstore glass to blockading the delivery vans that run to the fastfood joints, handing out flyers on the motorways and at every autogrill. We thought that since young workers were taking the brand of the neoliberal rules of work or the 'new flexibility' so to speak, and they have no memory of class struggle, we have to make it attractive. I am speaking about it but I am not the one doing it. You know, it's our graphic designers Karen and Zoe – who are behind the EuroMayDay website and the ChainWorkers webzine. So, it is to speak in a lingo that changes across time. I mean, youth language changes, youth aesthetics change, fads and fashions change. To market an idea of radical union activity, to see if it is possible to make radical unionism attractive to the masses. So we built a website, we created merchandising, we have a board game called Precariopoly, the netparade in which anyone could join (which rallied 20 000 people alone – almost as large as the actual MayDay). You know, traditional leftist organisations tend to dismiss this kind communication as beside the point. But today people form their identities through media before reality. So if you have an attractive medium, as we have managed to develop, you have a powerful tool of organising and activation. Through the website people have started connecting us and little by little we have built a network in Lombardy that became national and then transnational. It is about being focused and unafraid to market oneself to the unconverted. Because it is easy to convince the Anarchists, the Communists, Zapatistas, Situationists etc. The hard part is talking to the people that are suffering with their bodies but they have no way out because they have no cultural system of reference that enables them to rebel against a very repressive system. If you read about Wal-Mart, if you read what Mike Davis has to say about Wal-Mart or even what Business Week has to say about Wal-Mart. It is a system based on prison labour – this is the model of work and production in the department stores and big retail industries.

GP: You were saying before that the idea of organising around the theme of precarity is not to demand the mundane existence of the workers of the 1960s and 1970s. But you are using terms like 'fuga' or 'exodus' to talk about escaping from the whole production system. In what way do you think working around these issues will capacitate people to get out and not be working all their lives, having these shitty jobs?

AF: Being a labour agitator is already a better job...[laughter] but sorry if I am joking. The point is, over the last twenty years there have been many ideas of escaping ... for example, Deleuze and Guattari. But what we have seen, and Empire is clear about this, is that there is no external dimension to this system nowadays: it is either war or trade. There is no escape.

Although every individual does not define him/herself according to the job they do. I mean, you are an activist, you are a lover, you are a father, you are a Moslem, a Jew, a stamp collector. But you are not a worker, as in the 20th century. Yet paradoxically you work a lot more than your dad did. That's the point. You work a lot more than a car assembly operator in the 1960s and the 1970s. All the struggles to have paid vacations, to have the weekend off, to have universal healthcare etc are crumbling. Even in the Netherlands, where there is universal healthcare, if you are an undocumented migrant (and there are thousands) you are not going to have it. If you are a mentally diseased person you are going to end up homeless and you are not going to have health coverage. Exclusion is everywhere.

So you are thinking you're cool in this niche, in your social work identity. But in fact, you are doing a favour to system of neoliberal capitalism because you are not confronting power relations on the job where they matter most. And increasingly, given the absence of public social spaces, what is the last public social space left on earth? The work environment is where people meet, discuss, share, talk about politics, sex, lives, whatever. So we are talking about access but we are there the whole fucking time talking about something else – being elsewhere, with the internet, with our minds, but we are there. And with your cell phone, you are always a call away from your boss, when you are eating, when you are fucking ... and you have got to go because there is a call. This is precarity.

We have to emancipate ourselves from the fiction that we are not subject to class domination. Because we fucking are! What new forms do class domination take? It is not Lenin, it is not Rosa Luxemburg, it is not Trotsky. It is something else that together we are fighting and discovering through our conflict. This is what I regard as autonomy, another good concept.

Gavin Sullivan <gavin@greenpeppermagazine.org> edits Greenpepper magazine

Merijn Oudenampsen <merijn.o@gmx.net> is co-organiser of the Amsterdam Mayday and editor of flexmens.org web and print magazine

Greenpepper http://www.greenpeppermagazine.org is a magazine for social justice and environmental issues, a tool for groups working toward social transformation. It is conceived as an essentially participatory project and only exists through numerous collaborations and support

IS PRECARITY ENOUGH?

Before the precariat came the mass worker. Kidd McKarthy puts precarity in historical perspective and challenges those working around the term to overcome their reproduction of existing power relations

The ChainWorkers CreW's call, 'Chain+Brain Workers Unite!' is bold, brash, and necessary for a reinvention of first person politics in the work place, but while ChainWorkers and BrainWorkers both share precarious work environments and social conditions, the precise conditions of their exploitation are critically different. The word precarious is difficult to properly translate into English, as in English it has a purely negative meaning. Webster's defines precarious as 'dependent on chance circumstances, unknown conditions, or uncertain developments; b: characterised by a lack of security or stability that threatens with danger.' This definition is an accurate characterisation of the working conditions of precarious labourers and a stark relief to the post World War Two socio-economic guarantees. These guarantees of wages tied to inflation, health care, housing, paid time off, unemployment insurance, and pensions were given to those workers who were deemed necessary, like the factory or mass workers, but were not given to students, part-time workers, and housewives. The past 30 years have been marked by a removal of these social guarantees from all working classes, and the fight to both retain and go beyond them.

In the United States, because of weak social movements and strong state repression, the protections of the welfare state were never as thorough compared to other industrialised countries. The removal of these social guarantees is much more advanced and complete than in other industrialised states. In 1999, when the founders of the CreW traveled in the US, they saw first hand what the reorganisation of waged work and the destruction of social safety net looked like, and knew that other industrialised countries, like Italy, would soon follow in a similar direction. The

ChainCreW, composed predominantly of skilled media and technology workers and using the term 'precarious' to cover both skilled and unskilled labour, first organised in Milan as a web zine, and then expanded to include other actions and events. Since organising their first Mayday in 2001, they have used this day as their primary vehicle for defining and spreading their identity of precarity. I had the honour and privilege of working with ChainWorkers from the first meeting of 2004 to the first successful EuroMayday. In this article, I explain how the precarious identity was developed in both the Italian context and globally, and ask the question, 'Is the idea of precarity enough to honestly describe a wide variety of working experiences and bind us together to fight and to win?'

MAYDAY AS POST-MASS WORKER PROJECT

The project to dismantle the mass worker as the central object for labour struggles and place it on the shoulders of the more encompassing but diffuse idea of the precarious worker is an ambitious, yet necessary one. If we are to understand the precarious worker as a response to the mass worker, first we must understand the mass worker. The mass worker describes the generation of male, unskilled, assembly line workers of the gigantic factories that were first built in the 1900s but become ubiquitous after World War 2. In many places, Italy and the United States serving as two examples, this rise of the mass worker was accompanied by waves of internal migration from the rural south to the industrial north, and the firing of the female workforce that had entered the factories during World War 2. These massive factories, built for tens of thousands of workers, had many separate points of weakness that, when attacked concertedly, would halt the entire assembly line. During the global wave of struggles from roughly 1959-1977 factory workers were able to exploit these weaknesses. By using techniques such as checkerboard strikes organised on alternative days, lightning stoppages up and down the line, and the self-limitation of production, workers could collectively refuse to work, forcing factory bosses into negotiations.

From the mid-1970s, politicians and world leaders dismantled the controls imposed on capital by the Bretton Woods agreements', suspending the convertability of the dollar to gold (the gold standard).**1** With these controls gone and other shifts in the global economy, mass factories were replaced by smaller specialised factories, which were often moved to 'international' locations. New technologies facilitated automation in the factory and the factory worker became more disposable than ever before.

Taken together these shifts dramatically changed the nature of the factory-based labour force. Fewer workers were required, and the ability for these corporations to transfer operations and financial capital to other locations meant they were much less vulnerable to protest, attack, sabotage, and pressure from inside the factory than before.

With the overall decrease in the factory workforce, for the first time in generations, new generations would not be condemned to the factories, yet they faced the insecurity of having no guarantees of long-term employment or financial security. This insecurity and constant turnover was a dramatic change from working one job for thirty years, which not only provided a form of economic security but also a solid social identity. Once, the expectation was to get a job and keep that job or employer until retirement. Now, being part of a 'flexible' work force means having six or seven careers in a lifetime. Without an expectation that any of these jobs will be held for long, identity has become more grounded in life outside of work, life outside of work being both more self-managed and secure than waged work. It also meant that since workers are unable to disrupt production using classic methods, workers would have to develop new strategies to force factory owners and investors to negotiate and/or capitulate.

The destruction of the manufacturing base has been accompanied by the stagnation of wages and the rise in working hours. The United States and England are two telling examples. In the Unites States, the average two parent, middle income family now works 16 more weeks per year than in 1979**2**, and the workforce in the US in 2002 worked five more weeks a year than Germany.**3** 20 years after British Prime Minister Margaret Thatcher broke the miners' union, British workers now work more hours a year than anyone else in the European Union.**4** Yet, despite the destruction of the manufacturing base, the mass worker still remains the central figure in the work force in the western world.

THE ABSENCE OF A CRITIQUE OF SOCIAL POWER

The CreW lacks an analysis of power and how it functions across lines of race, gender, class, and sexuality. Because Italy is relatively racially homogeneous, issues of class and gender are of prime importance. Directly related to gender is the invisibility of domestic work. In fact, globally, most people are not even 'wage labourers', but actually work for no wages. Most people perform the work of basic work necessary for day to day living and social reproduction: cooking, cleaning, childcare, tasks that in other words encompass the wide range of basic labour that is usually considered 'woman's work'. No analysis of wage labour can be complete without an analysis of unwaged labour. This glaring blind spot colours solutions like a 'social wage' or 'income for all'.**5** Through the co-optation of feminist struggles in the 1960s and '70s, the home has been transformed from what was usually a place of patriarchal domination to what is now another site for wage labour.

BRAIN OVER CHAIN

BrainWorkers are creators, writers, artists, musicians, programmers; people who are hired not for their general labour but for specialised skills or their creativity. Though their time and creativity is stolen from them and sold back to us all as commodities, as software programs, movies, jingles, and advertising clips, they are more socially respected and able to command higher wages. In comparison to ChainWorkers, BrainWorkers have much greater control over their working conditions. The very nature of the work makes it impossible to Taylorise**6** and there is more flexibility at work to use the time directly as they wish. This is impossible for the ChainWorkers of Walmart, Starbucks, McDonald's, etc. They are automatons and the only thing they have to sell is their labour. With the introduction of computerisation and the commodification of all forms of information, an extreme form of rationalisation pervades the entire workplace: hamburgers are now measured in 15-minute blocks, and keystrokes are measured by the hour. For ChainWorkers, there is all the discipline of the factory with none of the interdependency and vulnerabilities which formerly allowed workers to fight back.

CONCLUSION

The CreW, being a very media-savvy organisation, has been able to change the terms of the debate about work in Italy. However, issues around social power remain formally unaddressed and despite the call for unity, BrainWorkers dominate the group. The CreW operates as a relatively closed group, intervening in the work place from the outside, encouraging workers to assert their rights and to make contact with the self-managed unions in Italy. Perhaps, instead of treating all forms of labour insecurity and exploitation as the same, it might be more effective for ChainWorkers as an organisation to empower chainworkers by transmitting its skills and tactics in creating media, so that ChainWorkers can control their own struggles. And, perhaps, we activists in the English-speaking world can join the debate around precarity and begin to grasp how waged labour has changed over the last 30 years, so we can challenge and destroy it.

This is an edited version, of a text that originally appeared on the website of Greenpepper Magazine

http://www.greenpeppermagazine.org/process/tiki-index.php?page=Contrarian+Article

FOOTNOTES

1 The Bretton Woods system of international economic management was set up at the end of World War 2. A chief feature was the maintenance of fixed exchange rate between currencies back by (US) gold reserves. [Mute editor: For a fuller analysis of the significance of the end of dollar-gold convertability see Michael Hudson's book 'Super Imperialism'. Free download at:
http://www.soilandhealth.org/03sov/0303critic/0303socialcriticism.html]

2 http://www.epinet.org/content.cfm/newsroom_releases_swa090102

3 International Labour Organisation:
http://www.ilo.org/public/english/employment/strat/kilm/kilm06.htm or CNN:
http://www.cnn.com/2001/CAREER/trends/08/30/ilo.study/

4 http://money.guardian.co.uk/work/story/0,1456,1256144,00.html

5 Dating back to the late '60s, the idea of a 'social wage' or 'income for all' was theorised by Italian far left groups to challenge the immediate hierarchies of skill and command found in wage labour and to uncouple income from productivity.

6 Taylorism or the theory of Scientific Management, is the theory that there is a most efficient way to do any task. In this view the workers are machines to be reprogrammed with better and more efficient instructions.

 Thanks to Alan and Steve. For their history and insights, written and otherwise

PRECARIOUS, PRECARISATION, PRECARIAT?

Impacts, traps and challenges of a complex term and its relationship to migration

By Frassanito Network

I. Precarious literally means unsure, uncertain, difficult, delicate. As a political term it refers to living and working conditions without any guarantees: for example the precarious residential status of migrants and refugees, or the precariousness of everyday life for single mothers. Since the early 1980s the term has been used more and more in relation to labour. Precarious work refers to all possible forms of insecure, non-guaranteed, flexible exploitation: from illegalised, seasonal and temporary employment to homework, flex- and temp-work, to subcontractors, freelancers, or so called self-employed persons.

II. Precarisation at work means a growing transformation from guaranteed, permanent employment to less well paid and more insecure jobs. On a historical and global scale, however, precarious work is not exceptional. In fact the idea of a generalisation of so-called guaranteed working conditions was itself a short lived myth of the 'welfare state' era. In the global South, in eastern Europe, as well as for most women and migrants in the north – altogether the great majority of the global population –, precarious working conditions were and are the norm. Precarisation describes moreover the crisis of established institutions, which represented for that short period the framework of (false) certainties. It is an analytical term for a process and hints at a new quality of societal labour. Labour and social life, production and reproduction cannot be separated anymore, and this leads to a more comprehensive definition of precarisation: the uncertainty of all circumstances in the material and immaterial conditions of life of living labour under contemporary capitalism. For example: wage level and working conditions are connected with a distribution of tasks, which is determined by gender and ethnic roles; residence status determines access to the labour market or to medical care. The whole ensemble of social relations seems to be on the move.

III. Precariat, an allusion to proletariat, meanwhile is used as a combative self-description in order to emphasise the subjective and utopian moments of precarisation. Through the mass refusal of gender roles, of factory work, and of the command of labour over life, precarisation has, in fact, a double face: it is possible to speak indeed of a kind of flexibilisation from below. Precarisation is not simply an invention of the command centres of capital: it is also a reaction to the insurgency and new mobility of living labour, and in this sense it can be understood as the attempt to *recapture* manifold struggles and refusals in order to establish new conditions of exploitation of labour and valorisation of capital.

Precarisation thus symbolises a contested field: a field in which the attempt to start a new cycle of exploitation also meets desires and subjective behaviors which express the refusal of the old, so-called fordist regime of labour and the search for another, better – we might even say, more flexible – life. However, we think that, as a new term of struggle, precariat runs into an old trap if it aims at a quick unification and creation of a dominant social actor. The Precariat has potential to become a farce, if, because of the increasing involvement of leftist activists in precarious labour and life conditions, the radical left tries to legitimise itself as the main force in its representation. But the real point is that, taking into account the hierarchies which shape the composition of contemporary living labour (from illegalised migrant janitors to temp-working computer freaks), the strong diversity of social movements and their respective demands and desires, nobody should simplify precarisation into a new identity. We are confronted here with the problem of imagining a process of political subjectivation in which different subject positions can cooperate in the production of a new common ground of struggle without sacrificing the peculiarity of demands that arise from the very composition of living labour.

In these conditions, we think that precarisation, as a complex and contested process, can offer a frame:

- to bring different subjects into an intensified exchange, on a social as well as on a political level;
- to mediate contradictions and even concurrences within respective realities;
- to pick out comprehensive questions as common themes.

We are thinking of a process based on the autonomy of various struggles, which fosters the communication between struggles, which invents new forms of cooperation and which opens new fields.

IV. Particularly because migrants experience all the above mentioned forms of depreciation and precarisation of contemporary work, and particularly because mobility is their answer through and against borders and identities, they manifest in their subjective conditions all the main characteristics which shape modern labour as a whole. In their subject position a common ground of the existence of social labour today finds a peculiar expression. To talk about migrant labour means to talk about a general tendency of labour to mobility, to diversity, to deep changes, which is already affecting – although with different degrees of intensity – all workers. Because of the possible extension of these conditions we speak of the political centrality of migrants' work. The position of migrants represents the social anticipation of a political option to struggle against the general development of labour as it is being extended to the whole of society and the whole life of all people. At the same time, we are aware that migrant labour as well as precarious labour doesn't represent a homogeneous subject: the process of subjectivation we are talking about is a process which must go through migrant labour itself, and which can be fostered by an increasing communication with other struggles and with the demands of other sections of contemporary living labour.

The Frassanito Network <frassainfo@kein.org> was named after an area in Puglia, Southern Italy, where a NoBorder camp was held in summer 2003. The network shares a conception of migration as social movement and sees migrants' struggles as crucial to the development of the whole global movement

MARX AND MAKHNO MEET MCDONALD'S

What does 'precarious' struggle look like in practice? Loren Goldner gives this account of casualised workers in Paris who, combining union and extra-union, legal and illegal tactics recently won several strikes and honourably lost another

Over the last several years, a revolving network of militants in Paris, France, have developed a strategy and tactics for winning strikes by marginal, low-paid, outsourced and immigrant workers against international chains, in situations where the strikers are often ignored by unions to which they nominally belong, or are actually obstructed by them.

While some of these methods benefit from aspects of French labour law that are more favourable to strikers than one finds in the backward US of A, the overall strategy can certainly find its uses in other countries.

The group, which calls itself simply Collectif de Solidarité (Solidarity Collective) slowly emerged as a network from the ferment and upswing in struggle following the 1995 near-general strike in France over pension 'reform'. Their composition ranges from casualised workers to people with steady jobs, people who want to fight and who see no perspective for doing so within a traditional union framework. Experience taught them that initially isolated strikes of marginal workers employed by big chains, in the worst possible conditions, can win if they are turned into city-wide actions by militants from 'outside' the workplace (but hardly 'outside' the increasingly downsized and outsourced work force), and (equally important), militants who are not members of vanguard groups coming mainly to fish in troubled waters for their own recruitment. The strategy could not be farther from the timid 'corporate campaigns' as developed by the likes of Ray Rogers, politely asking stockholders to sympathise with workers, but instead involve direct action to shut down businesses with a mixture of legal and 'extra-legal' (in the grey area between legality and illegality) tactics. The network also makes use, where and when it can, of better-known methods of creating embarrassing publicity for well-known corporate logos.

The current wave of activity took off in 2002 in a victory for a McDonald's strike in the heart of Paris. Five employees were arbitrarily fired, accused of stealing from the cash register. A strike of 115 days ensued, with regular support actions from other McDonald's and fast food restaurants around Paris. In this strike, one organiser from the restaurant department of the largest French union, the CGT (Confédération Générale du Travail), sensing an opportunity for some publicity, did help the strikers (who were members of the CGT), against the indifference or hostility of the rest of the union.

But the actions of the Solidarity Collective were indispensable in keeping up picket lines, turning away customers and explaining the strike to them, and occasionally shutting down other McDonald's locations around Paris. After nearly four months, McDonald's management caved, rehired the fired workers, and granted other concessions.

The committee then turned its attention to a struggle that became its greatest success to date, the 10-month strike of African immigrant maids at ACCOR, the third-ranking multinational hotel chain.

The Senegalese and Malian women involved were often barely literate, spoke little or no French, had never been informed of what rights they had under French labour law, and were subjected to killing piece rates based on the number of rooms cleaned. Further, their jobs were outsourced to a cleaning company, Arcade, with completely arbitrary scheduling based on the amount of work available from week to week. Most of the women developed work-related physical conditions after a couple of years on the job, which were not recognised as workplace injuries. They did belong to the small alternative union SUD (Solidarity-Unity-Democracy), but even this union mainly walked away from the strike early on.

In spite of these obstacles, the Solidarity Collective was able to keep the strike alive with unceasing 'pin-prick' tactics, disrupting hotel lobbies with leafleting twice a week, explaining the strike to hotel guests and putting pressure on customers and other hotel employees to support the strike; these and other highly visible interventions placed ACCOR and Arcade management on the defensive. Their main object was a (successful) attempt to disrupt the smooth impersonal functioning of the hotels and to expose the outrageous conditions of the maids to public view. As in the McDonald's strike, the Solidarity Collective provided the decisive forces that on occasion kept the strike alive even when most of the strikers were demoralised and close to giving up, while always being careful not to substitute themselves for the strikers. Benefit concerts made the strike more widely known and raised money. After 10 months, management again caved, most importantly on the crucial issue of piece rates, the pressures of which were significantly reduced. Further concessions were made in the introduction of regular scheduling, rehiring of fired strikers, and a payment of 35% of wages for the time struck. The only concession made by the strikers was an agreement not to make the contract public, so that it could not be used as a guideline in other situations. This did not, however, prevent the terms of the settlement from becoming widely known in the militant milieu. On the other hand, ACCOR was able to play on the secrecy of the agreement to make its application as difficult as possible, leaving enforcement in the dubious hands of the very union (SUD) that involved itself in the strike only at the end, to claim credit for the victory to which it had contributed next to nothing.

The experience of this strike in turn set the stage for further involvement in a renewed strike at McDonald's in Paris. As soon as management thought they could get away with it, they moved to fire and harass employees involved in the original strike. As a result, the struggle erupted anew in early March 2003.

What follows is a description of a few days' work by the Solidarity Collective in early May 2003. It attempts to convey the culture of direct action that is at the centre of its perspective, in which I was able to participate through a number of months.

Following the traditional march of an estimated 300,000 people in Paris on a not particularly spirited May Day, the Solidarity Collective managed to assemble 100 people for direct action against Frog Pub, a British chain with four restaurants in Paris, where 28 Tamil (Sri Lankan) kitchen employees had been on strike since mid-April. The group invaded the restaurant, confronted the manager and attempted to persuade the customers to leave.

On May 3, 30-40 members of the Solidarity Collective held a meeting in the occupied McDonald's restaurant in the Strasbourg St-Denis area of downtown Paris. We then marched to the nearest Frog restaurant about 10 minutes away. The strike of Tamil workers had begun in reaction against the firing of a Tamil assistant manager but that question was quickly overshadowed by demands over outrageous working and sanitary conditions and numerous violations of labour law. The boss assigned people their vacation time when it suited him; the dishwashers had to work with cold water; there was no extra pay for overtime; people getting off at 1 AM had to be back at 8 AM (whereas legally there are supposed to be at least 11 hours between shifts). The Frog manager had told one Tamil worker: 'I'm pleased with your work. A European wouldn't do it for even an hour.'

The pleasure of participation was heightened because a fair number of the Frog clientele were arrogant yuppies, many of them Brits, as was the manager quoted above, who became apoplectic. On this second intervention, the Solidarity Collective did not fool around. Here a certain 'strike culture' specific to France came into play, one not easily transposable to American conditions. People marched into the pub and immediately one spokesman started shouting through a bullhorn; within minutes the main door was blocked and covered by a 15-foot tape with strike slogans in 10 languages and a detailed leaflet in French and in English.

Then the police showed up and a bizarre ballet began. (One can only imagine the response of the NYPD or the San Francisco TAC Squad in a comparable situation.) They treated the strikers and strike supporters with kid gloves (it was generally assumed they were under orders to do so, in order to avoid episodes creating bad publicity for the right-wing Chirac government, just then gearing up for an attack on public sector workers), huddling with the strike supporters over a legal restraining order saying that pickets could do this, but not that, etc. We could block the main entrance, but not be inside persuading the customers to leave, and so forth. Periodically one of the strikers set off a bullhorn that sounded like a police siren, adding to the generally unravelling atmosphere.

Then we marched to another McDonald's that was also on strike. It was packed but it was shut down in about five minutes by the same tactics. We were turning people away at the door telling them the place was closed and 90 percent left immediately. It was particularly interesting to see lots of scruffy 'hip hop' types taking note of the strike.

At 6:30 PM the same day, a second action was undertaken at another Frog location in the very upscale Saint-Germain-des-Pres neighbourhood, on a little side street. For all the complications that later emerged between the strikers and the CNT (Confédération Nationale du Travail), the anarcho-syndicalist union they had joined, it was initially an upper to turn the corner and see the Tamil pickets with their red and black banners CNT banners, somehow symbolic of a real internationalism. Most of the Tamils barely spoke French and at times it was difficult to tell (through the lone interpreter) what they made of all the factional politics swirling around them, not to mention (as it later turned out) their own factional politics (cf. below) Nonetheless, as union members in the anarcho-syndicalist CNT, they were protected by all kinds of labour laws that don't exist or are a dead letter in the US: they couldn't be fired for striking, they couldn't be permanently replaced by scabs (but could be replaced by temps during the strike itself), and if they returned to work they would be protected by their open-ended contract. Nevertheless, public support for the strike was impaired by a widespread overestimation of the efficacy of these laws, and an underestimation of the need for direct action to tip the balance of forces.

The locale was hardly a 'proletarian' scene, with mainly upscale foreign tourists and French bourgeois passing by. The Solidarity Collective managed to get a fair number not to cross the picket line, and some of us were explaining the strike to people in English, French, German and Spanish. With an old shoe box, we started collecting money and raised about 30 euros ($35) in 2 hours. This is a great crash course in sociology, seeing who responds and who doesn't. It was also interesting because even people who were obviously indifferent or hostile were polite. I imagined similar types in the US telling me they were damn well going to eat where they pleased. That said, it must be pointed out that the specific climate leading up to the imminent showdown over public sector pensions in May-June 2003, definitely increased sympathy for the strike among passers-by and potential patrons.

The Solidarity Collective has developed these tactics in 5-6 strikes of the most exploited immigrant and young French workers in the Paris region and the tactics often work. The collective is made up of a Paris-wide network of militants who see the need to go beyond workplace-organising; the decisive elements in winning such strikes are 30-40 people from outside the workplace who give, or try to give the strikers the forces they need for all the aspects of waging a strike that gets into trouble, above all through isolation. At the same time it's not 'Leninist' in that no one is there to recruit people to an organisation. The Collective aims to put the strikers in charge of their own struggle in a way that neither a union nor a typical leftist group does. It has as its sole aims the victory of the strike and the deepening of the 'flying picket' network available for the next battle.

What kind of reservations can be articulated about the kind of roving tactics of the strike support group? They obviously don't solve 'all' problems, and the Collective itself recognises that its ability to turn away customers at the door made for the special vulnerability of the locales in which they were successful. The Collective is the first to recognise that far greater numbers would be necessary to stop a plant closing or to paralyze a military machine.

But these tactics do create something like a small-scale version of the Toledo Auto-Lite strike (1934), in which other members of the precarious labour force turn isolated losing strikes of the most downtrodden (immigrant) workers into something that really hurts management, both in the pocketbook and in terms of their reputation. It responds at least partially to the great success of management in atomising resistance at the 'point of production' by having a rapid turnover of teenagers, etc. It turns the management success of the last 20 years on its head; the latter's intent was to create a precarious constantly recycled temporary work force that would never be around long enough to organise at the work place, and here is that same work force showing up 'outside' the work place to shut down business and enforce conditions for some of their number. Today's strikers will be tomorrow's pickets at other sites, or they will be strikers at other sites. Recycling thus cuts both ways by downsizing but also in freeing groups of workers from corporatist attachment to lifetime jobs and making them into potentially roving pickets supporting necessarily roving workers. Further, it solves the problem of union indifference or obstruction; it uses unions where possible for legal protection but circumvents unions when they ignore, or worse, obstruct a strike for some instrumental end of their own. It tells unions to put up or shut up, and when, as in most cases, they do the latter, it uses a mixture of legal and illegal tactics which unions (at least in the US) would never dare attempt. It circumvents the Labour Notes-type strategy of ingratiating oneself with the left wing bureaucrats or of becoming left-wing bureaucrats; the Committee takes the initiative while not waiting for the unions to do so. In a comparable situation in the US, a typical union would show up, set up its own skeleton picket line, tell 'outsiders' the matter was none of their business, and honour whatever injunction some judge hands down. Finally, unlike various front organisations set up in the past, Solidarity Collective people are NOT a vanguard group fishing for members in troubled waters; they come as equals in the recycled labour market.

Beginning in May, 2003, the Frog Pub strike began to be transformed by the large public sector strikes that began in March and continued until the end of June. For weeks, Paris saw one (mainly controlled) mass demonstration after another. The main issues (which can only be dealt with in the most summary way here) were the government's (ultimately successful) attempt to increase the work requirement for full retirement benefits for public employees to the 37 years already in effect for the private sector, and to attack teachers with a series of educational 'reforms' aiming at large-scale layoffs of non-academic personnel and the reorganisation of curriculum in accordance with the 'local' job market.

The Frog strikers, many of whom were cooks by profession, hit upon the idea of selling drinks and sandwiches to the passing demonstrators from strategically-located sites along the demo route, combined with the aggressive publicity for the strike and fund-raising which the Solidarity Committee was conducting in every demo already. This tactic netted the strike fund a much-needed boost, and just as importantly made the strike against the 'patrons negriers' (slave-driving bosses) known on a scale unimaginable in its initial phase.

At the same time, it must be said that the series of mass demonstrations, mass meetings and occasional confrontations with the police totally dwarfed the forces of the Solidarity Collective, and created a situation in which the traditional leftist vanguards, above all Lutte Ouvriere, could successfully carry out their systematic takeover and manipulation of the mass assemblies. In spite of numerous independent rank-and-file initiatives, the unions and the leftist groups ultimately were able to do their work of demobilisation well.

Even before the mass movements faded away, however, several factors began to weigh on the Frog pub strike, and, in contrast to the successes of the initial McDonald's strike and of the African maids against ACCOR and Arcade, set the stage for a defeat, one for which, however, Frog management paid a steep price on several fronts.

The first unfavourable turn of events was an internal crisis of the CNT that directly undermined the Frog strike. Little enough is known outside the union about this internal crisis, which unconscionably turned the strike into a factional football among CNT mini-bureaucrats, except that at its culmination it led to the summary replacement of the head of the CNT's restaurant section. Instead of largely ignoring the strike (as the CGT, with one notable exception, had done with McDonald's) or walking away and then claiming responsibility for the victory at the end (as SUD had done with the African maids' strike), the CNT initially ran the strike with little attempt to involve the strikers, presenting themselves as 'professionals' who would made short shrift of Frog management in a few weeks.**2** The upshot of this method, when this bravado was revealed for the empty pretension it was, led the strikers to see as their only reliable allies the Solidarity Collective, which latter the CNT was treating as nothing but an organisational rival, projecting their own gate-receipt mentality onto the Collective's intentions. In the final months of the strike, only a handful of CNT militants continued to work seriously with the strikers and the Solidarity Committee.

Taking a similar destructive toll was the discovery, in mid-summer, that 7 of the strikers were members of the nationalist Tamil Tigers. One of the two Frog Pub managers had managed to contact the Tigers, who constitute a sort of shadow government for the 15,000 Tamils living in the Paris region, much as the North African Islamic fundamentalist groups attempt to impose themselves on the North African population in France. Through whatever deal or payoff, the Tamil Tigers not only pulled their own members out of the strike but threatened the life of one of the strikers who refused to give up.

By mid-summer, the public sector and teachers' strikes had largely been defeated, except for the ongoing actions of the intermittents du spectacle **3** that continued sporadically into the fall.

Nonetheless, the work of the remaining 7 strikers and of the Solidarity Collective began to bite, particularly at the largest Frog pub at Bercy, whose clientele had seriously diminished in sympathy with the strike, a situation prevailing well into the fall.

As a result, in spite of the fadeout of the CNT and the 'intervention' of the Tamil Tigers, the Frog managers were still keen to settle. Finally, in October 2003, the remaining strikers accepted a lump sum payment of 5000 euros each in exchange for being laid off (which would qualify them for further unemployment benefits).

This article, in sum, has as its intent making these tactics and these successes and failures known to militants outside France. Nor should it be misunderstood as any kind of triumphalism. As indicated, Collective members are acutely aware of what they can and cannot do with their small numbers, and of the specific vulnerabilities of the types of employers where their tactics have succeeded. Further, in the wake of these struggles, management has returned to the offensive. Only a year after their first defeat, as recounted, Macdonald's attempted another provocation and took a long second strike; the ACCOR hotel chain is harassing the maids who struck, firing one of the most militant and visible militants, and a new campaign by the Collective is underway. From other quarters of defenders of elements of the status quo, some leftist groups have had the effrontery to accuse the Collective of manipulating the strikers, whereas a refusal of substitutionism has always been one of its distinguishing features.

Transposing these tactics to US conditions will obviously have to take account of the significantly rougher terrain they will confront. But I am aware of no other approach, in confronting the employer offensive now underway for more than three decades that has had anything like the Solidarity Collective's small, but still impressive successes.

FOOTNOTES

1 I wish to thank Nicole The and G. Soriano, whose camaraderie in extended discussions during the events of 2003, made this article possible. It further benefited from a close reading and criticisms by Nicole The. Also cf. Note 2 below.

2 For readers with a knowledge of French, the article of G. Soriano 'L'experience des collectifs de solidarite parisiens: une nouvelle etape', in La Question Sociale (No. 1, 2004) offers a much more detailed analysis of the Frog strike, and of all the machinations of the CNT. This publication can be contacted at laquestionsociale@hotmail.com.

3 The 'intermittents du spectacle' were culture workers in the arts and media who, until 2003, who eligible for minimally-livable unemployment benefits between jobs. The government's overall attack on public sector pension rights and teachers also eliminated this programme, though the 'intermittents' continued their struggle for months after the other strikes had folded. For an overall analysis of the strike movement of 2003 in France, cf. the Echanges et Mouvement pamphlet Pour une comprehension critique du mouvement du printemps 2003 (September 2004). BP 241, 75866 Paris, Cedex 18, France.

Loren Goldner is a writer and activist living in New York City. Much of his work is available on the Break Their Haughty Power web site at http://home.earthlink.net/~lrgoldner

DISOBBEDIENTI CIAO

Hydrarchist analyses the death of the Italian extra-parliamentary political network, Disobbedienti (Disobedients), and reports on the rise of social precarity as a focus of political action in Italy

No formal announcement certified the end of the Disobedients (Disobbedienti) in Italy but the once dominant extraparliamentary network's demise seems scarcely in dispute. What originated as the 'White Overalls' (WO) alliance between groups in the Veneto, Rome and Milan in 1998, encompassing satellite groups in other cities, is now in full decomposition as its constitutent elements abandon the logo and reassume identities related to their everyday territorial reality. The consequences are manifested both in a reshuffling of the relationships between the movements and the political parties, and a plurality of campaigns as the focus of struggle. But first some background and explanation.

The widespread riots and fierce police repression that accompanied the G8 in Genoa dealt a mortal blow to the model of controlled conflict and hybridisation with other political forces that had constituted the WO project since 1998. A language of heightened confrontation was adopted prior to the G8, but the scale of state reprisals found them unprepared. Afterwards there was a failure to assess what had really happened, as each group attempted to distance itself from responsibility. But repression can also produce unity and trans-regional ties were galvanised between some of the fractious inheritors of Autonomia Operaia (where a strong Rome Padua axis can be traced to the late '60s), the youth section of Rifondazione Communista (RC– an offshoot of the old Communist Party and still a major force on the reformist left) and the Greens around a platform of 'social disobedience'. Thus occurred an apparently seamless transition from White Overalls to Disobedients, presented as a laboratory for experimentation with new political forms rather than a proposition for any type of unitary organisation. Nonetheless the new network suffered numerous defections due to exhaustion, unhappiness with the way in which Genoa had been managed, and from a sense that the open and experimental spirit which fuelled the WO had now disappeared. From this point onwards the Disobedients would be perceived as a force threatening to hegemonise and erode the autonomy of other groups. Their national nature, media-presence and involvement with political parties made them easy to cast as imperialist and overbearing.

Apart from a shared hostility to the suffocating and disciplinary pressures of the Communist Party there have always been radical differences in the autonomist left as to the attitude to assume towards elections. From 1976 some 'extraparliamentary' groups ran candidates on the list of Democrazia Proletaria (absorbed by RC in 1992). Participation was justified as a means to construct counter-power and extend the dynamic of conflictuality to these institutions. Others assumed an abstentionist position, rejected mediation and advocated social autonomy – the daily unfolding of material conflict in perpetual antagonism to politics, understood as an institutionalised management of social conflict.

The Disobedients were perceived as threatening to hegemonise and erode the autonomy of other groups

Relations with the parties vary according to local factors, which in Italy can never be underestimated. In the Veneto (Padua, Venice) acute hostility towards the Communist Party tradition combined with the evisceration of concentrations of labour in the factories – the Veneto's restructured economic form based on small-scale networked production has made it a textbook example of post-fordism – and the importance of environmentalism have made the Greens the post-autonomists' political vehicle of choice. Being a 'salon' party with neither tradition or a consolidated grassroots, the Greens are less resistant to new ideas, more malleable to internal reconfiguration. The relationship has allowed the translation of the autonomists' strong territorial presence into an increased political visibility and thus provided a greater margin for action. There are concrete benefits as well: the stability of occupied spaces; the ability to create structures with which its militants can survive materially; and legitimation through a role in local government.

Meanwhile in Rome the chaotic urgency of the metropolis produces self-organised reappropriation for the resolution of basic needs, especially housing. RC remains an important force in the city and contains significant pro-movement elements. Here the Disobedients have reformed around ACTION (Agency for Social Rights), driven by activists from the social centre Corto Circuito, which has won accomodation for more than a thousand people through occupations and earned considerable respect. Since 1997 they have also elected city and district councillors as independents on the list of RC, a relationship which extends their capacity to negotiate over housing and provides protection from otherwise certain police prosecution. In both Rome and the Veneto work with migrants for housing and papers has been central in recent years – and this extends to libertarians and activists of all stripes – and has been an area where intervention at an institutional level is both useful and inevitable.

FRACTURE

Tensions over the relationship with the political parties came to a head in the Disobedients during the European elections in June. Whilst the Veneto section supported the candidacy of the Greens' Bettin, the Romans ran a popular candidate on the list of RC, Nunzio D'Erme, famous for having dumped several bags of manure in front of Berlusconi's Roman residence. Polling better than expected, he was their fifth highest vote-winner nationally. RC's share of the vote gave them five seats to distribute but D'Erme was passed over in favour of Niki Vendola, from the South where the RC are currently enjoying considerable growth. Given that a candidate from the North-East was given a seat with a far smaller number of votes, this was understandably viewed as betrayal, and evidence of a cynicism towards the movements to which it had professed an openness since the mid-'90s. This crisis polarised existing divisions within the Disobedients and political bloodletting on a local level lead to a reversion to local identities and a retreat from hybridisation. RC are now openly in cahoots with the government-in-waiting of Romano Prodi, whose Grand Democratic Alliance will challenge and probably defeat Berlusconi at the next election. Consequently the radical left needs to reposition itself with respect to the future power structure, both to get what they need and retain a clear oppositional profile.

Nonetheless some type of relationship with the political system remains unavoidable, even if unformalised or unwitting. How one conceives the purpose of representation will fashion the terms on which it occurs. One vision explicitly legitimises local politics as a space to establish a counterweight to the deterritorialising tendency of globalised production, and a stage for practical demonstrations of counter-government. Here parallels are made with Zapatista autonomous communities, which, transposed to Italy, has meant involvement at a municipal level and the election of councillors. Elsewhere Antonio Negri recently set out criteria for the relationship with party politics in general, insisting on the absolute primacy of the social movement over political parties, whose legitimation resides solely in their capacity to serve, resource and open up political space for extra-political activity.**1** Accordingly, party alliances are justified provided that the relationship is not one of subalternity (whereby parties exploit social movements so as to rebuild their diminishing base) but 'navigational' authority, where party direction derives from demands expressed externally. Handily enough this both functions as a justification for the past as well as a programme for the future, and an argument for keeping RC at arms length.

In the meantime the rapid rise to prominence of social precarity as a political flash-point has seen an influx of former Disobedients (now rebranded as 'Invisibles' and 'Global') into the organisation of the Mayday parade in Milan.**2** A derivative network named PreCog – precarious and cognitive workers – has taken shape in the last year, popularising the cult of San Precario, mythopoetical patron saint of dispossessed but combative subjects, with the intention of rejuvenating the popular imagination of a fight for new social rights. As a network PreCog contains many sensibilities external to the former Disobedients including a 'Neurogreen' tendency (environmentalist and libertarian with a focus on imposing pressure at local and European level) which sees in the Green Party a vehicle for more flexible political opposition and a global environmentalist sensibility proper to the problems of advanced capitalism. Meanwhile the social autonomy perspective within PreCog and the the 'National Network for a Guaranteed Income', which continues to prioritise the diffuse conflictuality of the 'precariat' and its ability to configure the social balance of forces, is also in a process of growth and recomposition.**3** In spite of these heterogeneous approaches the outline of a shared trajectory emerged around the question of income, encompassing the national demonstration for a guaranteed income on 6 November 2004 and next year's Mayday Parades.

Some type of relationship with the political system remains unavoidable, even if unformalised or unwitting

THE PRECARIAT STRIKES BACK!

The simmering tension between parties and movements came to a head during the November demonstration. Under the playful acronym GAP – Grand Alliance of the Precarious, a parody of Prodi's Grand Democratic Alliance – workplace committees from Alitalia to care-workers, grassroots trade unions, and social centres of every hue converged for direct actions of reappropriation to protest the increasing cost of living and demand access to wealth and a street parade through the city centre. 'Autoreduction' is an Italian term for imposing a discount 'from below' and it was planned to perform one in a suburban supermarket. Having neutralised police attention through cunning use of the subway system, the protestors arrived eventually in Pietralata, immortalised in Pasolini's films *Theorem* and *Accatone*, where a shopping centre owned by Berlusconi is handily located by the train station. Once inside 700 participants filled their trolleys with goods, and blocked the cash registers chanting 'everything costs too much!' Negotiation began with management for a discount of 70 percent for everyone in the store, but in the meantime many people simply walked out with their trolleys and began distributing goods to families and pensioners, drinking wine and sharing sweets. This gesture was initially met with incredulity, but soon the party was in full swing. Meanwhile the electronics and clothing departments upstairs were by now in the grip of frenzy: computers, phones, DVD players and flat-screen monitors made their way out the door. At this point many 'ordinary shoppers' had succumbed to repressed desire and started to help themselves. Faced with a plainly uncontrollable situation the small number of police present were powerless. Later that day it had been planned to distribute copied DVDs inside the Feltrinelli book and entertainment chain as a symbolic rejection of copyright laws that limit access to culture and knowledge. Echoes of the morning however were too strong; as the demonstration passed by 200 people entered, filled their arms with books and charged back out into the street into the street parade of 25,000 people: workers committees, migrants, grassroots trade unions, house occupants and students, and a hundred other shades of precarity.

700 participants filled their trolleys with goods, and blocked the cash registers chanting 'everything costs too much!

Predictably the media and political class have embarked on a hysterical condemnation of these actions, and have attempted to impute responsibility to the Disobedients, who as recounted above scarcely exist. Arrests and a 'zero-tolerance' policy have been promised. Notwithstanding the brouhaha, commentators have had to acknowledge both a widespread sympathy for what happened and the emergence of the precariat as a problem henceforth at the centre rather than the margins of society.**4** Individual MPs from both the Greens and RC have even expressed support, but the parties have officially distanced themselves from the acts, widening the schism between movement and orthodox forms of representation. RC's current fixation with consensus and terror at any taint of illegality that could be depicted as being violent makes constructive cooperation nigh impossible. Here no violence was involved and the action was performed without any attempt to conceal participants' identities, a fact for which participants will pay a heavy legal price.

Amidst all this however, GAP has maintained a tortured silence, torn between the need to respond whilst under the public eye and the distrust of collective utterance and representation which remain unresolved. Journalists have filled this void by nominating former Disobedients as the voice of the precarious. This unhelpful personalisation derives from their use of 'spokespeople' – in fact leaders – that monopolised media coverage of the 'no-global' period. Such distorted representations allow the action to be pigeonholed as belonging to pre-fabricated media constructions – 'autonomists', 'Disobedients', 'inheritors of '77' – cast as alien to people's everyday experience of contradiction with their living conditions, and so inhibiting any broader social identification with the practice.[5]

A renewed realism as to the acute difficulties faced in everyday life underlies the emphasis on precarity. Spiralling rents, an increased cost of living, and poor social/labour mobility – not to mention the apocalyptic turmoil worldwide – are generating a pervasive sense of uncertainty about the future. In the absence of a substantial social welfare buffer, this focus enables a narration of needs and desires in the first-person and facilitates a rupture with discourses of the 'no-global' period which often lapsed into a jaded third-worldism, where the 'serious' problems were often exoticised or abstracted as somebody else's, somewhere else.

Social movements in Italy function best when external factors oblige cooperation and marginalise intra-movement rivalry, yet an inability to coldly appraise the efficiency of discarded strategies threatens to nullify the benefits of experience. The Gordian knots of representation, relations with the institutions, and internal and network democracy are not going away. With a centre-left government on the horizon, and the fertile ground for reactionary demagogy that promises, the challenge will be to maintain abrasive contestation, autonomous from the party system, without being relegated to the margins, where the only dividend is unceasing police attention.

FOOTNOTES

1 Antonio Negri, 'Contro il pensiero molle dell'organizzazione', Posse, Nuovoi Animali Politici, Manifesto Libri, April 2004

2 http://www.globalproject.info and http://www.euromayday.org

3 See http://www.incontrotempo.info

4 For a good introduction to the politics and cartography of precarity, see Green Pepper's issue devoted to the theme. http://www.greenpeppermagazine.org

5 Hierarchical political action remains prevalent in Italy, a fact often missed

Hydrarchist is a researcher and contrarian

WAGES FOR ANYONE IS BAD FOR BUSINESS

Venezuela's 'Bolivarian constitution' contains a unique article (Article 88) recognising women's unwaged work as economically productive. Wages For Housework (WFH) has been fighting for this recognition since 1972, and has particpated in the annual Global Women's Strike (GWS) since its inception in 2000. GWS members attended Venezuela's international 'Solidarity Women's Encuentro' in July 2002, and saw women at the heart of the revolution and its social changes. Laura Sullivan spoke to Selma James and Nina Lopez of WFH and GWS

WFH believed 'women had a right to money of their own', says James, 'because the power relations between women and men, and in fact all power relations under capitalism, were distinctions of wages and a hierarchy in production.' She and her colleagues fought for that money to remunerate the unwaged work of women the world over, meeting some resistance, for example, accusations that WFH was founded because Jewish people like James 'are only interested in money'. James scathingly lambasts the liberal women's movement. She contends that feminist critics neglected to understand that women – already institutionalised in the home – only have 'two ways to go: they can either get money from the state, or go out and get a second [i.e., waged] job.' 'Women [who went into the male workforce] were absolutely rolled over – the feminists orchestrated it, praised it – they didn't see women were being rolled over, and they complained women weren't getting equal pay. They also asked for "non-traditional jobs" for women. When the first woman was killed in the mines, I was very angry.' The politics of women's liberation endorsed by the WFH, then, starkly contrasts with a fight for women to enjoy the same capitalist exploitation and oppressive conditions as men.

James explains that when others were 'disconnecting production, which was the production of value and surplus value, from reproduction, which was making human beings', WFH declared that 'housewives and other carers were part of the working class,' that is, women's unwaged labour was productive in the Marxist sense because it contributes to the reproduction of labour. [see inset box] Disgusted with the 'many idiots' who said that women in these unwaged positions were outside of capitalism, James emphasises that WFH 'is an organising movement,' while 'all those who opposed it, organised nothing – they didn't say, "We'll do this instead".'

A similar emphasis on practical effectiveness underpins the work of GWS in Venezuela. As James and Lopez tell it, when a CIA-backed coup took place in the country in April 2002 and president Chavez was kidnapped by the opposition, the women 'saved the revolution' when they came down from the shanty town neighborhoods in the hills around Caracas 'and demanded that Chavez be released. Everyone was in a state of shock. The women insisted that the military do something. The military, who were largely loyal to Chavez, went and got him back.'

Through its newspaper, talks, demonstrations, and videos, the GWS counters media misinformation and silence, documenting Venezuela's revolutionary achievements, such as Bolivarian schools and circles, land redistribution, progress in health care and literacy, as well as women-centred efforts. The GWS sponsored a US tour by Nora Castañeda, president of the Women's Development Bank, which helps 'women living in poverty become independent protagonists in the revolutionary struggle',**1** particularly through financing thousands of co-operatives. Castañeda emphasises that the daily pressure of women and indigenous people on the Constituent Assembly was crucial to the passage of Article 88, which declares that women's work in the home is 'productive', that is, 'creates value' and entitles women to social security (i.e. pensions, education, and health care), and Article 14 of the Land Act, which gives women heads of household priority in land distribution. A March 2004 GWS letter to the National Assembly urges the full and honest implementation of Article 88. Other priorities, such as the recent referendum recall vote, have delayed its implementation.

Until recently, Lopez explains, the left was largely uninvolved with and unsympathetic toward Venezuela. Traditional Marxists saw Chavez as problematic because his base was primarily in the unwaged sector, 'rather than at the so-called point of production.' James contends that Chavez is 'married to the movement, to the grassroots,

Emma Ortega
Coordinator for the movement for agricultural reform
Only at a local level can nutritional
sovereignty succeed in overcoming

Argelia Naguanagua de Ramos
because we don't have any water.

All pictures > Stills from the film *Venezuela from Below*, by Dario Azzellini and Oliver Ressler, 2004

which he thinks is central – as Marx did – as the left does not.'

James contextualises the relationship between Chavez and his followers: 'It's not the first time in history that the movement has related to a leader as a saviour – people did to Lenin, who wasn't totalitarian. In the same way, black people related to Malcolm – he could do no wrong.' James views access to power as the pivotal issue: 'When people find a leader who wants to lead them where they want to go, the intellectuals are shocked – they just have no grasp of how it feels not to have power and then somebody who has a bit of power and wants to go in the direction you want to go and take you with him – they don't know how that feels, they haven't been without power.' James and Lopez emphasise people's involvement in the Venezuelan government, whose 'constitution speaks of the people as protagonists of the democracy, aiming for people to represent themselves.' Chavez is 'an organiser, totally practical, connected to the grassroots. His military background is useful – civilians don't know how to run a government.' Chavez applies his disciplinary skills to all levels of governing, including the recent election, in which volunteers telephoned ten people to discuss candidates and to encourage voting. In a month and a half, the whole country was organised in such a fashion, with a 73 percent turnout! Boldly and practically devising 'a basically foolproof electoral system (knowing that the big problem was to avoid fraud),' Chavez demonstrated his 'big trust in people's organising abilities, particularly women, who were the majority in the neighbourhoods and helped folks to vote.' The election was peaceful because it was well organised and centrally involved women.

Women – already institutionalised in the home – only have 'two ways to go: they can either get money from the state, or go out and get a second [i.e., waged] job'

I wonder how to reconcile James' emphasis on the role of women and the celebration of the revitalisation of grassroots politics with the focus on the president, a top-down form of power, as opposed to spelling out that the ultimate goal is the end of representational politics altogether. In other words, women are identified as political levers in the revolutionary process in Venezuela, but to what end? Is their horizon ultimately antithetical to the goals of Chavez, who, after all, must not only work to stay in power but who has also been increasingly complying with neoliberalisation (i.e. the concessions he's made post-coup)? Chavez is undoubtedly a unique leader very much in touch with 'the people': for the progress of women and all Venezuela's disenfranchised it is presently essential that he stay in office. Yet isn't there still a contradiction between

Chavez's position as a charismatic leader in a hierarchical system, and the WFH goal of the *destruction of hierarchies*?

While the GWS women are clearly in sympathy with the goal of overthrowing capitalism globally – and to their credit, more involved on the ground with poor women, women of colour, and 'third world' women than most academic or other feminists – their anti-intellectualism manifests in static theorisations (starting and ending solely with the unwaged/waged distinction and the fight for women to receive wages for all their labour in the home) and their lack of a real plan for how this strategy fits in with the broader field of struggle against capitalism. When I asked, 'what succeeds wages?', the question was not at all well received. In the first instance it was misunderstood to mean 'What do women do once they get these wages?' (met with the hostile response of 'You wouldn't even think to ask this question of men'), and in the second, seen as an overly theoretical concern about whether a movement or strategy is 'anti-capitalist' versus seeing what it accomplishes on the ground, in people's lives. Calling the question itself 'inappropriate', James challenged, 'If you see workers on a strike demanding a 25 percent rise, is it for or against capitalism? Your problem is that you haven't made up your mind about wages for anyone – capital has. Wages for anyone is bad for business. If you waver, you decide that you don't care if capitalism is hurt, you care if [your strategy] is anti-capitalist.'

Women are identified as political levers in the revolutionary process in Venezuela, but to what end?

At the same time, frustration with perceived strategic or theoretical shortcomings should not lead left intellectuals and activists to dismiss totally the efforts of groups such as the GWS and the women they champion in Venezuela. We should continue to learn about and understand the context – the political and material urgency – that informs such efforts. Making an easy critique from outside, the 'anti-hierarchy' 'pro-decentralisation' left cannot account either for the popularity of leaders such as Chavez and Castro or for the dialectical relationship between such leaders and state structures *and* socialist policies, practices, and projects that make a real difference in people's lives (e.g., Cuba's continued 98 percent post-revolution literacy rate; the redistribution of land and wealth underway in Venezuela). Without doubt, the implementation of the remarkable Article 88 will make a great difference in the lives of many Venezuelan poor women of colour, and we should appreciate an organisation such as the GWS, which publicises and furthers such policies.

My investigation of the history of the WFH campaign became an unanticipated detective effort. The essay that undergirds the work of WFH, 'Women and the Subversion of the Community,' is often cited from a 1975 booklet as being co-authored by Mariarosa Dalla Costa and Selma James; however, James's introduction to this collection refers to the 'Dalla Costa article'. And yet a note added by the 1975 publishers (the Power of Women Collective) insists the essay was jointly authored, claiming Dalla Costa publicly admitted this many times. However, not only has Dalla Costa told me James's name was added to the essay without her permission, the first, 1972 English publication of the essay in this booklet lists only one name: Dalla Costa. Perhaps these conflicting attributions reflect not only the split between James and Dalla Costa – who did not sign on to the WFH campaign – but also the essay's more pressing contradictions over whether seeking wages for housework is appropriate.

On the one hand, having made the case that 'domestic work' is a 'masked form of productive labor' (36), the essay concludes that 'the demand that would follow, namely "pay us wages for housework" ... could scarcely operate in practice as a mobilising goal' (36). On the other hand, an endnote seems to make the opposite case, arguing that 'the demand for a wage for housework is only a basis, a perspective, from which to start, whose merit is essentially to link immediately female oppression, subordination and isolation to their material foundation: female exploitation. At this moment this is perhaps the major function of the demand of wages for housework' (54).

FOOTNOTES

1 Interview with Nora Castañeda, Global Women's Strike newspaper, No. 2, November 2003, page 3

Laura Sullivan <alchemical44@yahoo.co.uk> is a writer, digital artist and counsellor, leading workshops providing emotional support for activists, amongst others

$
£
fr
¥

CALL TO ARMS

In the summer of 1999 Kolinko, a group of German radicals, decided to start working in call centres, examining exploitation there and strategies for overcoming it. Three years later they published *Hotlines*, an invaluable document for those wanting to understand how work is carried out and resisted in call centres. The group have been criticised by some for promoting workers' enquiry as a political project and engaging in 'radical sociology'. Here, Kolinko reprise and defend the thinking behind their research, and one member gives a first hand account of his time working at one of the largest call centres in the UK

A RADICAL ENQUIRY

The *Hotlines* book describes a three year process of enquiry in call centres, attempting to understand the situation there, workers' behaviour during and against work, conflicts, and interventions – through leaflets and otherwise. In this enquiry, we saw ourselves as workers participating in the struggles and trying to support their development. We had a guiding principle: make clear to other workers, and ourselves, the actions that are already being carried out. Our goal was not to enlighten 'unreflective' workers, but to push beyond our own limited horizons.

We do not believe in the supposed separation between workers and militants/activists, one lot with their crazy revolutionary ideas, the other only interested in more money and job security

We want to grasp the standpoint of the collective social worker: the effects of technological change, the impact of the social and international division of labour on everyday life, the experiences of other workers in their struggles, and the power they develop through them. It's about breaking up the limited perspective which the isolating capitalist organisation of work imposes on us, blocking our own view of things.

Of course, our attempts to get an overview, to understand class conflicts, and to throw our ideas into discussion – in other words, the ways and means we use for enquiries – ask for a continuous debate. We used the *Hotlines* questionnaire mainly for reflecting our ideas and for starting discussions with other workers. Consequently there was much they missed; it did not say much about struggles in other sectors, about crisis, and nothing about war. Better leaflets would draw the lines between the events on the shop floor or in the job centres and the global transformations of capitalism – a means to further encourage discussion among workers by supplying information on other struggles. In the worst case, they won't read that

stuff or know what to do with it; in the best case they will use it during upcoming conflicts and start to spread their own experiences through leaflets or other media.

We do not believe in the supposed separation between workers and militants/activists, one lot with their crazy revolutionary ideas, the other only interested in more money and job security. While there may be thousands of examples of the 'individual worker' – individualism and competition while searching for a job, demands in collective bargaining situations, racism against newly emigrated workers – there are also many examples of the opposite: the doctor's receptionist who does not want to work in medical practices any more even if she gets paid better, because she prefers being together with larger numbers of workers in a call centre; the casual worker who doesn't give a shit about money and security and goes surfing after four months of work. Historically there are many examples of workers who act against their economic interests – enjoying themselves by burning down their company, killing the boss and so on.

Enquiry is one method that can be used in order to understand this space between workers' behaviour as labour power that wants to improve its conditions, and as the class that wants to put an end to exploitation. It can do this by dealing with real processes, contradictions, and tensions. Workers already make enquiries: they are interested in the wages of their foremen, conflicts in other departments, the restructuring management has planned (sometimes even in the struggles of the landless in Brazil or the unemployed in Argentina); if they don't make such enquiries, they lose out, unprepared for the next conflict. In most cases the division between those who are interested in what's going on and those who are not is not a division between so-called 'revolutionaries' and workers, but between workers themselves.

Workers already make enquiries: they are interested in the wages of their foremen, conflicts in other departments, the restructuring management has planned (sometimes even in the struggles of the landless in Brazil or the unemployed in Argentina)

For us the issue of our exploitation corresponds directly with that of our struggle. We don't have to tell anyone that we/they are exploited: it's a collective effort to understand the social dimension and structure of how this exploitation is organised. We have no desire to be militants or activists, sacrificing ourselves for a historic mission, getting on everyone's nerves including our own. Rather we make this choice: to deal with the situation collectively, rather than individually, whenever we have to sell our labour power or cope with the worsened conditions at job centres and the welfare office. For instance, we can decide together in which places of exploitation we want to earn our cash and at the same time participate collectively in conflicts. That way, our disgust for the capitalist daily routine and our anger against the conditions and those who oppress and exploit us can flow together into one common political project.

Enquiry is the condition, form and method of our attempts to understand the current struggle and to take part in it. Those who would still like to go into these questions in more detail from the perspective of our experiences should read the *Hotlines* book.

http://www.nadir.org/nadir/initiativ/kolinko/lebuk/e_lebuk.htm

LONDON CALLING

I had heard a lot about call centres, day after day, for two years. I thought I knew what to expect.

THE COMPANY

One of the biggest market research companies in the world. They have offices or call centres in 36 countries, big multinational or government clients. For example the Australian General Union asked the company to conduct a survey about flexible work-time. They should just have asked the company's workers – they knew all about it already.

THE CALL CENTRE

The call centre is in London, near London Bridge, in a side street facing a high red brick wall with barbed wire on top. A group of young Spanish and Italians stand in front of it, the Italians swearing about Berlusconi, the Spanish smoking weed. Two doors, one pincode, then you are inside the 'postmodern chicken farm' as people call it. Packed little phone booths for hundreds of interviewers. The job is market research, phoning people in France, Italy, Spain, Germany, the UK, Ireland, randomly selected by the computer. At the end of each row, the supervisors' desks.

THE CONDITIONS

The whole thing started with two days' unpaid training, basic brainwashing about market research, how to use the antique computer program and so on. The second day a really nice guy from French Reunion Island came in ten minutes late and was sent home again, unpaid, but at least only half brainwashed. The stylish gay Asian supervisor, who regularly handed out anti-globalisation information and was a very welcome guest at various call-centre-workers' parties, was able to justify giving him the sack.

After these two days you can start working – if you get your shifts. You have to book them a week in advance and if there is no work, you won't get any. The management wanted to introduce a new shift scheme, with a top list of interviewers: whoever completes the most interviews, whoever has got the least 'idle time' and is the most punctual and obedient worker can choose their shifts first. If you are a miserable worker, you'll get what's left over. Theoretically you can book as many shifts as you want – of course there are some legal restrictions, but they don't really count. I saw people working 12 hours a day, seven days a week, although that's a sad exception.

THE WORK

If you press 'y' after the computer asks you 'another interview?', it starts dialling random numbers. When you are lucky, you get connected to a fax machine or a modem and you can press '8', just to be asked the same question again. In between '8' and 'y' is the kingdom of idle time, but watch it – the king or queen of idle time gets into trouble. If you are connected to another human being you have to start asking questions.

Most sensible people hang up after hearing the word 'market research'; all the others usually are very lonely, mentally unstable or just wrong in thinking they're doing you a favour. We do surveys about alcoholic drinks, fast food chains, mobile phone networks, DVD-players and digital cameras, cars, petrol stations, post offices and more. We do it every day, 'til nine in the evening.

Imagine phoning a small Irish village on a Sunday night asking about DVD players. At least you can hide behind your script. You are supposed to read it from the screen, word for word. How else could you possibly think of questions like 'Imagine Burger King is a person with its own personality. Would Burger King be introverted, bold, immature or warm-hearted'? The average interview takes about 20 minutes, on average you do three to four interviews in a four hours shift, the fruit of 200-300 phone calls. Rumour has it that the company gets £70 for each interview.

THE WORKERS

From all over the world, in their 20s, most of them 'creative' in one way or the other. It would be wrong to say that they are 'students', though most of them have been. You can talk about Guy Debord with a French female artist just back from Cuba, the drummer of an anarchist Italian hardcore band, a gay second generation Turkish boy from Cologne who is studying fashion design, a traditional Asian Muslim man from the East End, a girl from a village in the Alps with a population of fifty, who just arrived in London – all in a four-hour shift. I've never worked in a place before where people were so critical and verbally able to dismiss their work, even capitalism as such. But I have also hardly ever seen people accepting such mind-numbing work and patronising management behaviour. Because it's just a job for a while? Because they mainly did that kind of job after quitting school or university? Because of the week-to-week shift system? I still don't have a clue why.

THE SUPERVISION

There is one supervisor for ten to twenty interviewers, monitoring the idle time, counting interviews and attempts, listening to what you say and how you say it. They come to your desk if you are not dialling for five minutes; they give you bad marks if you don't stick to the script. They walk around and tell you to put your book or newspaper back into your rucksack and to bring the coffee back to the coffee machine, because hot drinks are not allowed. For an extra pound an hour and the privilege of not having to be on the phone they wear themselves out.

THE SABOTAGE

It starts with small things. Little drawings or scribbles in each phone booth. A lot of 'Leave your brain at the entrance' stuff. Someone is constantly stuffing the toilets with toilet rolls, so the management put out these notices: 'Whoever is putting paper down the toilets, please stop it. It is unnecessary, unhygienic and causes inconvenience for everybody.' The next day people cross out the 'It', replacing it with 'Market Research', or the name of the most hated supervisor.

We started collective slam poetry, handing on poem lines from neighbour to neighbour. Sometimes we used the computer as well, pressing the right combination of codes to keep the computer dialling, assuming that there are only fax machines at the other end. But that's risky: the supervisor could be monitoring you. Sometimes, especially with lonely elderly people, we live out our social worker tendencies, talking about gardening and the new priest in the community, instead of fast food chains. Some Spanish guys developed a funny threesome, using the headset, passing the receiver on to the neighbour, so that the confused respondent talked to two interviewers. We faked management instructions that are placed in every phone booth, calling for the return of the Idle-Time King and mass orgies.

Imagine Burger King is a person with its own personality. Would Burger King be introverted, bold, immature or warm-hearted?

On Saturday shifts there is a higher drug consumption. That's when most of the weird stuff happens. Receivers at the supervisors' desks glued to the phones, people pretending to be preachers or radio show presenters. But there was never a real collective action. Once on a Saturday, 15 minutes before the end of a nine-hour shift, the supervisors circling to make sure we keep on dialling, some French girls suddenly started to cheer and applaud like crazy. All the pent-up energy broke loose and the whole call centre joined in, then packed their stuff and left five minutes early. We were never able to repeat that.

THE END

In the end, after six months, I got my fair share of disciplinary meetings, but wanted to leave anyway. It was my first and last call centre job. I found interesting people there, situations of solidarity and flirtation, a real friend. In political terms I am less sure. Maybe the most radical thing would have been to elect a shop steward or get rid of the zero-hour contracts and arbitrary management behaviour. But what for? To tie people even closer to this madness, by offering proper contracts? By that measure it would have become clear that we are workers with rights and our own interests. But why channel energy into such formally correct work relations, when there is all this disgust towards this kind of work, all this pent up creative anger?

What I missed here was a group of more experienced people, politically and job-wise, with whom to reflect on the situation. At first I thought a leaflet, for example about the new shift system, would be kind of 'external', so I just talked to my neighbours, made little drawings, like everyone did. But maybe something on paper, demanding a collective action and handed out to everyone would have forced all of us to define a position. Who knows..?

Kolinko's writing and research can be found at the website http://www.nadir.org/nadir/initiativ/kolinko/engl/e_kopre.htm